MORE THAN
BRAVE

GLENN HASCALL

MORE THAN
BRAVE

180 DEVOTIONS & PRAYERS FOR BOYS

BARBOUR **kidz**

A Division of Barbour Publishing

Published by Barbour Publishing, Inc., 1810 Barbour Drive, Uhrichsville, Ohio 44683, www.barbourbooks.com

Our mission is to inspire the world with the life-changing message of the Bible.

 Member of the
Evangelical Christian
Publishers Association

Printed in the United States of America.

001129 0322 SP

INTRODUCTION

You are brave—or maybe you're not. You stand up when it would be easy to pretend you were invisible—or maybe you don't. You get your strength from Jesus—or maybe you're still curious about that.

This book is all about next steps. It will encourage you to be brave enough to discover all the things you needed when you weren't very brave. But you don't have to stop at bravery. There is more to life than that, but bravery is the start you need.

It will be hard to live a life that is filled with things like purpose, kindness, honesty, and wisdom if you're never brave enough to talk to the God who wants to give them to you as a gift.

You will be asked to think about what you can do to co-operate with God. He can take your bravery and use your willingness to do things you could never do on your own. Bravery doesn't make you a superhero, but it does give you the chance to walk with God on an adventure He created just for a brave boy like you.

So stand tall, be brave, show courage. You're going places.

TAKE STEPS

When the Christians heard of our coming, they came to meet us. They came as far as the town of Appius and to a place to stay called the Three Stores. When Paul saw them, he thanked God and took courage.
ACTS 28:15

Paul needed courage. You wouldn't know that if the Bible didn't tell you. There was a time when Paul didn't like Christians. Not one bit. Most people only knew Paul as the guy who hurt Christians. But that's not what God saw in Paul.

Today's verse is about a time when Paul followed Jesus, knowing that most people couldn't believe he was a Christian. Yet in this story there were Christians who wanted to meet Paul. They knew God could change people. This helped Paul to be brave. This was a moment when Paul took a step beyond bravery. That's where he needed to be. That's where you need to be too. Keep reading, and in the words you read you'll find that it's good to take steps to the place where you're more than brave.

- -

I NEED TO BE BRAVE FIRST, LORD. YOU CAN HELP. THEN KEEP HELPING ME TAKE EACH NEW STEP AS A BRAVE BOY.

THE STRONG STAND

Be strong with the Lord's strength.
EPHESIANS 6:10

God will never ask you to be strong on your own. No one is that strong. Not a movie star, football player, or any other human. They never have been. They aren't now. They never will be.

If you're looking for the perfect role model, you won't find one on earth. Oh, there are good ones. Some people are great examples of what it looks like to wear God's strength, but it's God who gives that strength. On their own they are weak, and they will tell you so. The best examples are weak people who honor God for making them brave, strong, and courageous.

They are the kind of people who do everything they can to stand up for what they believe, and then when they know they are getting weak, they keep standing, waiting for God to show up. When God gives what only He can give—and you accept what only He can offer—it shows you may be ready for His next gift.

- -

I AM WEAK, GOD. YOU ARE STRONG. I WILL STAND. HELP ME KEEP STANDING. HELP ME FOLLOW WHEN YOU MOVE.

A BETTER CHOICE

May the Lord Jesus Christ be with your spirit.
May you have God's loving-favor.
2 TIMOTHY 4:22

God wants you to be brave. He wants you to believe you can do more than you thought because He can be *with your spirit* and He can show you His *loving favor*. Keep this knowledge close and understand how important it is; God is a friend who doesn't leave or abandon you. He doesn't make fun of you or criticize. He doesn't discourage when He redirects you to a better choice.

Brave boys admit when they're afraid, and they take their fears to the God who has never been afraid. That's when they can let go of fear. Without fear, bravery becomes possible.

Then brave boys can pray today's verse for others. You will want Jesus to be with others. You will want God to show loving favor to others. Brave boys don't keep the secret to bravery to themselves.

- -

I NEED TO KNOW AND ALWAYS REMEMBER THAT YOU'RE WITH ME, FATHER GOD. YOUR LOVE HELPS ME STAND WHEN I WANT TO RUN AWAY. HELP ME TO BE BRAVE. THAT'S JUST WHAT I NEED TO BE.

9

BRAVERY BELIEVES GOD

"Be strong. Let us show ourselves to have strength of heart. . . . And may the Lord do what is good in His eyes."
2 SAMUEL 10:12

The words in today's verse were spoken by Joab, the commander of King David's army. He didn't always make good choices, and he wasn't always remembered as a nice guy. But he was helping soldiers during battle. Enemy soldiers were facing them and coming behind them. That's when Joab spoke. He encouraged the soldiers to be brave. He told them to remember that when the battle was over, it would be because God did "what was good in His eyes."

If they were going to make it through this battle, it would be because God showed up to help—and He did!

Joab was reminding the soldiers that bravery believes God can do the impossible for people who ask Him for help.

Think about the most difficult thing you've ever experienced. Did you let God help you? Did you have strength only God could give? What will you do differently next time?

- -

HELP ME TRUST YOU ENOUGH, LORD, THAT WHEN BAD THINGS HAPPEN, I BELIEVE YOU'LL TAKE CARE OF ME.

BIGGER THAN YOUR FEAR

Since God is for us, who can be against us?
ROMANS 8:31

What if you could live your life knowing that there's nothing and no one who can stand against God? What if you could remember that God is for you and encourages you? What if you absolutely believed that when you follow God, no one who can stand against you?

This doesn't mean you'll never have trouble. It means that when trouble comes, it has to do what God tells it to do. What may seem scary is that sometimes God allows trouble to bother you for a while, but He never lets trouble win. *Never.*

Being brave means you're convinced that God is bigger than your fear and stronger than your trouble and can deliver confidence when you have questions.

God can give you strength to get through trouble. Whatever you face, God faces with you. He answers your call, so *don't forget to call.*

- -

YOU ARE GOD, AND YOU ARE FOR ME. WHEN I'M
WITH YOU, I'M PROTECTED AND I'M LOVED. WHEN
I'M WITH YOU, I KNOW THERE'S NOTHING TO FEAR.

YOUR GREAT RACE

Even if I walk through the valley of the shadow of death, I will not be afraid of anything, because You are with me. You have a walking stick with which to guide and one with which to help. These comfort me.
PSALM 23:4

This is a book about how God uses bravery to help you learn many other things. It helps you to be strong enough to trust in God's better plan.

If bravery is your starting point, then that means that you've been courageous enough to begin walking with God. But as you turn each page, you'll begin to discover dozens of ways you can be brave and make a choice to follow God in new and exciting ways.

You can do that without fear because He guides you and helps you. Be satisfied in knowing that everything you need is just what God is willing to give.

You can be more than brave, but bravery is the starting line of your great race.

- -

FATHER, WHEN I STRUGGLE WITH CHOOSING BRAVERY, HELP ME TO REMEMBER THAT THIS IS WHERE YOU HAVE CHOSEN FOR ME TO BE WHEN I GET SERIOUS ABOUT FOLLOWING YOU.

FEAR OR FAITH

[Jesus said,] "Why are you afraid? You have so little faith!"
MATTHEW 8:26

In today's verse, Jesus was sleeping in a boat when a storm came up. The disciples were overwhelmed. Some probably thought they would die. Jesus simply told the storm to calm down, but before He did, He spoke to the scared disciples, saying, "Why are you afraid? You have so little faith!"

These men needed the faith to believe that Jesus could rescue them. They let a storm stop them from belief. Jesus reminded them—and you—that fear always fights for the same place as faith.

Bravery can be the very thing that helps you accept God's offer of rescue. When it's hard to believe that God loves you enough to rescue you from the choice to break His law, you need a way to reconnect with God. You need courage to find faith.

Faith is the trust you need to believe something is true even when it's hard to explain—like the quick ending of a powerful storm.

- -

I NEVER WANT TO LET FEAR STAND IN THE WAY
OF FAITH, LORD. IT'S EASIER TO DO NOTHING THAN
TRUST YOU, BUT I NEED TO TRUST YOU.

FAITH, BELIEF, TRUST

Jesus put His hands on their eyes and said, "You will have what you want because you have faith."
MATTHEW 9:29

Blind men came to Jesus. They wanted to see, and they knew Jesus performed miracles. If they were ever to escape darkness, they would need His kind of miracle. That's what they wanted.

People did not treat them well. They probably felt like they were always in the way. They knew that some people would make fun of them for asking, but they really believed Jesus could heal them. So they sought Jesus, they asked, and they waited for a response.

The bravery that led to faith also led to an answer from Jesus: "You will have what you want because you have faith."

When you pray do you have that kind of faith, belief, and trust? Are you convinced that Jesus can help you? Jesus looks for the kind of faith that knows there's no other source for answered prayer.

- -

YOU ANSWER PRAYERS. HELP ME BELIEVE IT, FATHER. YOU WANT WHAT'S BEST FOR ME. HELP ME BELIEVE THAT. YOU HAVE ALWAYS LOVED ME. GIVE ME THE FAITH TO ACCEPT THAT.

THE GIFT OF FAITH

You do not have faith in Christ because of the wisdom of men. You have faith in Christ because of the power of God.
1 CORINTHIANS 2:5

The real bravery you experience is a gift from God, but He didn't stop there. That bravery leads to another gift—faith. That gift is yours because God is more powerful than your fear and doubt.

God can overcome all the things you're uncertain about. He can cause faith to grow where mistrust once thrived. God doesn't want you to live in a place where you believe nothing good will ever happen. He doesn't want you to think that doubt is the perfect response.

You won't be convinced because you read it in this book. You believe because God helps you learn enough to believe, to be rescued, to accept His love.

God can use things like this book to cause you to think about Him, but He will be the One who offers you the gift of faith.

- -

YOU'RE THE GOD WHO GIVES GOOD GIFTS, FATHER. HELP ME BELIEVE THE TRUTH ABOUT YOU. HELP ME ACCEPT THE GIFTS YOU'VE ALWAYS WANTED ME TO HAVE.

HE WANTED TO HELP

I live by putting my trust in the Son of God. He was
the One Who loved me and gave Himself for me.
GALATIANS 2:20

When you're asked to do something in your family, how willing are you to do what you're asked? Do you go out of your way to be helpful? You might struggle with being helpful. Other things might seem more important to you.

Jesus loved you so much that He made the decision to do everything needed to help you in the best possible way. Jesus never claimed to be too busy to help. He never said that he couldn't help because you might be selfish sometimes. He wanted to help you before you ever asked for help.

Every day you're given gifts. You have water to drink, food to eat, air to breathe, and people who love you. The good gifts offered to you also include forgiveness and a forever life. Brave boys choose this life.

- -

YOU MAKE ME BRAVE, AND THEN YOU OFFER GIFTS I
DIDN'T EVEN KNOW I NEEDED, FATHER. HELP ME ACCEPT
WHAT YOU OFFER AND WALK WHERE YOU LEAD.

GIVING UP

[Joshua said,] "As for me and my
family, we will serve the Lord."
JOSHUA 24:15

Joshua was brave. He would lead the people of Israel into the land God had promised, but the people he led weren't sure God was worth following. You probably know that was a bad decision, Joshua knew it was a bad decision, and God knew it was a bad decision. The people thought it was a better idea to believe whatever they wanted and follow whoever seemed interesting.

Joshua knew he needed to talk to the people about these bad choices. God took the people away from slavery and was giving them a new home, but that didn't seem to matter. Joshua wanted them to think about whether it was a poor decision to follow God after all He'd done for them. Then Joshua bravely told them that his family would follow God. That speech made sense to many of the people. They were brave too. They gave up a bad choice for the best one—following God.

- -

HELP ME TO BE BRAVE ENOUGH TO FOLLOW YOU
AND THEN LET OTHERS KNOW WHAT I'M DOING,
FATHER. LET THIS BE MY BEST CHOICE.

YOU CAN TOO

Jesus said to him, "Thomas, because you have seen Me, you believe. Those are happy who have never seen Me and yet believe!"
JOHN 20:29

Thomas was a disciple. He followed Jesus, but he was a skeptic. That meant he found it hard to believe things until someone could prove them true.

When Jesus died and rose from the grave, He came and spoke to the disciples. Thomas wasn't there at the time. When the other disciples told Thomas that Jesus was alive, he told the disciples that he wouldn't believe Jesus was alive unless he saw His wounds. That wasn't brave. That wasn't faith. Jesus said so.

Thomas struggled to believe that what Jesus said was true. Jesus loved Thomas and showed Thomas His wounds so that he could believe. Jesus said that no one, including brave boys, needs to see Him to believe.

The good news is Thomas did overcome his doubt. He believed. You can too.

- -

LET ME USE MY BRAVEST MOMENTS TO BELIEVE IN YOU, GOD. LET ME USE MY COURAGE TO TELL OTHERS I BELIEVE IN YOU. LET ME USE MY CONFIDENCE IN YOU TO HONOR YOU IN THE CHOICES I MAKE.

BIG PLANS

The mind of a man plans his way,
but the Lord shows him what to do.
PROVERBS 16:9

Do you know what purpose is? Purpose is the biggest thing you're supposed to do. It's the reason you're alive. Some people never take the time to figure out what they were created to do.

God knows exactly what that is even when all you can do is guess. God also knows how each choice you make can either move you closer to that big thing or further away.

Don't be afraid to make big plans about what you'll do when you grow up. God said you would do that. What you really need to remember is that no matter what you plan to do, God can introduce directions that keep you from wasting time going to unhelpful places. When you follow Him, you get to the thing you were born to do faster.

A brave boy like you works with God to do the thing He knows only you can do.

- -

YOU PLANNED AN INCREDIBLE TRIP AND OFFERED TO GUIDE MY TOUR, LORD. I JUST NEED TO BE BRAVE ENOUGH TO ACCEPT YOUR OFFER. HELP ME TO BE THAT BRAVE.

BOUGHT

God bought you with a great price.
1 CORINTHIANS 6:20

Do you buy something with no plans of using it? It could happen, but not often. You buy a video game to *play*, right? You don't just hang it on the wall because you like the cover. You buy a bike to *ride*, not to sit in the garage. It doesn't make any sense to buy something you won't use.

God bought you. Jesus gave His life for you, and He wants you to accept new life in Him and see what God plans to do with the life He paid for. God bought you because He has plans for you. He bought you from slavery and set you free. He gave you new life so you wouldn't have to keep living the way you had always lived. He bought you because He has a purpose for you.

God's purpose is always more important than your past. His plan for your life is better than your plan. His patience lasts longer than yours. You will need God's purpose, plan, and patience to do what He bought you to do.

- -

SIN OWNED ME, BUT YOU BOUGHT ME BACK, FATHER. THANK YOU FOR MAKING IT POSSIBLE FOR ME TO BE USEFUL.

THE PLAN. A PROMISE.

The Lord of All has planned, and who can keep it from happening?
ISAIAH 14:27

If God makes a plan, do you try to talk Him out of it? Would it make sense to try? God knew everything before anything happened. He knows what you will say before you say it. He knows what you're thinking. God knows what needs to happen, and He knows what He wants you to do to help.

God doesn't spoil the surprise either. He has big plans, but you shouldn't be surprised if you only know enough to take one step at a time. That way when you finally arrive at one of the places He's made for you, it's like taking off a blindfold. You're amazed at how far you've come and where He has taken you.

Think about this: God made a plan to fulfill a purpose, and He didn't leave you out. He didn't say, *"Sorry, I can't use you."* He didn't even tell you that other people were more important.

- -

YOU AMAZE ME, GOD. COULD I REALLY BE SO IMPORTANT TO YOU THAT YOU HAVE A PLAN FOR MY LIFE? THANK YOU.

HIS WORK

We are His work. He has made us to belong to Christ Jesus
so we can work for Him. He planned that we should do this.
EPHESIANS 2:10

The best story started with "In the beginning God," and ends with "Let it be so." God created plants, animals, and people. He created you. Before the first man ever broke God's law, God had a plan to rescue people. When anyone is rescued by God, they become part of His forever family.

You get to make choices that look like what God is teaching you. When you help others, you're doing the work God does. It's exactly what He wants you to do. Will you do it?

Does your heart beat with bravery? Does it ask God, "What can I do next?" Maybe it sits alone, refusing to be brave while holding on to fear. Learn all you can about God's plan, and then say the very last words of the very last book of the Bible: "Let it be so."

- -

I WANT TO BELONG TO YOUR FAMILY, LORD. I WANT TO WORK FOR YOU AND DO THE THINGS YOU'VE PLANNED FOR ME TO DO.

NOT EVERY CHOICE

*Not everything is good for me to do! Even if I am free
to do all things, I will not do them if I think it would
be hard for me to stop when I know I should.*
1 CORINTHIANS 6:12

God has a reason for what He does when He makes plans for you. Let's take a look at some of the reasons you have for following His plans.

Not every choice leads to something good for you. Not every food is good to eat. Not every liquid is good to drink. Not every game is good to play. Not every show is good to watch. Not everything is good. That's why you have choices to make.

You follow God's good plan for your life by resisting those things that aren't good for you. When you make the choice to spend most of your time doing stuff that makes you feel good, then you might find yourself doing things you find hard to stop doing when you know that's exactly what you should do.

- -

IF I HAVE A CHOICE TO FOLLOW YOU OR DO ANYTHING ELSE, HELP ME TO FOLLOW YOU, FATHER. HELP ME SEE YOU AS THAT IMPORTANT.

WHATEVER YOU DO

*So if you eat or drink or whatever you
do, do everything to honor God.*
1 CORINTHIANS 10:31

Brave boys know that God has a reason for what He does. They even know that they have a reason for following. But today's verse uses three words to help you remember that the choices you make should honor God. The three words? "Whatever you do."

Following God isn't a part-time job. It's not something you do when you feel like it. It's not even something you do for a while to see if you like it. He loves you. Follow Him.

Today you read an answer about what you should be doing when you take your bravery and make it available to God. You take responsibility for *whatever you do* and ask God to help you make every choice a celebration of God's goodness to you and others.

- -

IT'S EASY TO BELIEVE I'LL ALWAYS MAKE THE RIGHT
DECISIONS, LORD, BUT I'LL NEED YOUR HELP. IT'S EASY
TO THINK I'LL HONOR YOU IN THE CHOICES I MAKE.
HELP ME LEARN TO MAKE GOOD DECISIONS.

24

TWO THINGS

Honor God and obey His Laws.
This is all that every person must do.
ECCLESIASTES 12:13

It's possible to think that God wants you to do certain things. But when you don't really know if what you're doing is what God wants you to do, then you could be wasting your time and getting no closer to God's adventure for you.

For instance, you can read today's verse and discover that some of the things you might be doing to get God to notice you may not be the things He wants you to do. And doing what you want to do isn't obedience at all.

There are two things God wants brave, faith-filled Christians to do: honor Him and do the things He tells you to do. That means you will need to read the Bible to find out more about what He wants you to do.

- -

THE BIG QUESTION I HAVE TO ASK MYSELF IS WHETHER I TRUST YOU ENOUGH TO DO WHAT YOU WANT, FATHER. YOU HAVE REASONS FOR THE THINGS YOU WANT ME TO DO AND THE THINGS YOU WANT ME TO AVOID. HELP ME TO BE BRAVE ENOUGH TO OBEY.

CLOSER

*[Jesus said,] "Why do you call Me,
'Lord, Lord,' but do not do what I say?"*
LUKE 6:46

You can believe God is pretty wonderful—and you'd be right. You can also refuse to follow His commands—the rules He wants you to follow. They include rules about not lying, stealing, or cheating. And there's more.

Jesus saw people who thought His miracles were amazing, but they hurt other people with words, thought they were better than most people, and wanted God to choose them over anyone else. Jesus said something that might sound like this today: "You say I'm worth following, but when I tell you what you should do, you ignore Me." When it sounds like that, it also sounds like you only like Him some of the time. That's not nearly enough.

To obey means doing the things that bring you closer to God. Forgiveness brings you back from a bad decision to a very good God.

- -

YOU HAVE RULES, FATHER. I DON'T WANT TO IGNORE THEM. I DON'T WANT TO ACT LIKE IT DOESN'T MATTER IF I BREAK THEM. HELP ME TO REMEMBER THAT JESUS DIED TO PAY THE PRICE FOR MY BAD DECISIONS.

FRIENDSHIP WITH GOD

Adam did not obey God, and many people become sinners through him. Christ obeyed God and makes many people right with Himself.

ROMANS 5:19

Obeying can be hard. Sometimes you don't want to do what you're asked to do. Sometimes you think the person who wants you to obey is just being bossy. Sometimes you just want to do what makes you happy.

Adam chose not to obey God. He thought God was trying to keep him away from something good. When Adam sinned, he introduced rebellion to the world. Everyone would follow Adam's example and sin. Jesus came to set things right. He obeyed God and never sinned. He was perfect. Then He died. God took Jesus' perfection and made it possible for sinners to be forgiven. Jesus' example makes it possible to see obedience to God as the best first choice.

Jesus did what Adam never could: He obeyed perfectly. And His obedience made a way for us to be friends with God.

YOU DON'T ASK ME TO DO ANYTHING JESUS DIDN'T DO, LORD. HE OBEYED AND WILL HELP ME OBEY. HE FORGIVES, AND SO CAN I. HELP ME SAY YES TO WHAT YOU WANT ME TO DO.

NO TROUBLE SLEEPING

*[Jesus said,] "Those who hear the Word
of God and obey it are happy."*
LUKE 11:28

Have you ever had trouble sleeping because you made the wrong choice, knew it, and couldn't stop thinking about it? When you obey, you don't have to worry about getting caught because you haven't done anything wrong. You don't have to lie about it. You never have to feel bad about making a good choice.

Obedience leaves you satisfied. Maybe it's because you're learning more about what God wants. When you know what He wants, you can do what He asks. When you do what He asks, you can experience a peace and calm you can't even begin to explain.

Some of the worry that you feel may have something to do with moments when someone disobeyed. Maybe that was you. Maybe it was someone you know. You are concerned because you know something is very wrong. Pray, tell God what you did, and be forgiven. Then? Make the choice to obey.

- -

IF I CAN DO WHAT YOU ASK, I CAN BE SATISFIED
KNOWING THAT YOU'RE TEACHING AND I'M
FOLLOWING, GOD. LET THAT BE MY CHOICE.

28

DOESN'T LOOK LIKE NEW LIFE

Be like children who obey. Do not desire to sin like
you used to when you did not know any better.
1 PETER 1:14

Some people break God's rules because they don't know what God's rules are. They may not know much about God, Jesus, sin, or forgiveness. But when you make the choice to do what God says because you follow Him, then you also need to think and act in new ways.

Brave boys begin to train. Like with football, they learn from their coach. They study the basics. They follow the game call. God says you can be successful, but you'll need to use your training and depend on His guidance.

Today's verse says you can learn. You can turn your back on bad choices. You can know better. This is exciting news. This means that things change for Christians. They are rescued, they train, and they recruit. Disobedience just doesn't look like your new life. And everything that God commands will leave you satisfied when you obey.

- -

HELP ME SEE OBEDIENCE AS PART OF NEW LIFE, FATHER.
LET ME SAY, "I WILL," WITH MY WORDS AND ACTIONS.

LOVE AND OBEDIENCE

Loving God means to obey His Word,
and His Word is not hard to obey.
1 JOHN 5:3

Maybe you've heard someone say, "You're not the boss of me!" They usually say this because they don't think anyone should be able to ask them to do anything. You might have said that to a brother, sister, or friend, but you'd never want to say that to God. He said that doing what He asks is the best way to show that you love Him. When you tell God no, it sounds a lot like selfishness. It might seem like you don't trust God. You might believe He doesn't know what He's doing.

Today's verse says that God's Word is not hard to obey. So that means a brave boy like you won't cheat, lie, or steal when God says not to do those things. He'll help. He always has.

- -

IT CAN BE HARD TO KNOW WHO TO TRUST, GOD, BUT I WANT TO TRUST YOU. THE BIBLE CAN TEACH ME A LOT OF THINGS. WHEN I LEARN ABOUT SOMETHING YOU WANT ME TO DO OR NOT DO, HELP ME OBEY, BECAUSE I'M LEARNING TO LOVE YOU.

THE DIRECTION OF RIGHT LIVING

My children, let no one lead you in the wrong way.
The man who does what is right, is right with God
in the same way as Christ is right with God.
1 JOHN 3:7

When a brave boy obeys God, he's considered righteous. That means that you do the right thing. You pay attention to what God wants, and you change direction to follow Him. When you let God lead, you learn what advice is worth following and what advice is worth turning away from.

Some people are very willing to lead you to a place that is different from where God would lead. You'll need the wisdom God can give to know what advice to accept. You'll also need to be brave, because when you follow God, that means you don't want to follow others. They probably won't like that.

Yes, obey your parents. Follow God. That's two steps in the direction of right living.

- -

RIGHT LIVING MEANS MAKING RIGHT CHOICES, FATHER. I WANT TO LEARN WHAT THOSE CHOICES ARE FROM YOU. I WANT TO KEEP WALKING WITH YOU. WHEN I DON'T, HELP ME TO BE BRAVE ENOUGH TO COME TO YOU FOR HELP.

RIGHT QUESTIONS

Happy are those who are faithful in being fair
and who always do what is right and good!
PSALM 106:3

What does it look like to be righteous? Let's take righteousness to school. Imagine someone picks on someone you know. You like both people, but that means you may need to pick sides. Do you approve of the bullying or stand up for the one being bullied? What is fair? Which is right? You might even need to ask yourself if you are happy with the choice you made.

God stands up for those who are picked on. He wants to rescue those who have no friends. He wants you to do the same thing. The Bible says that God loves those who are picked on and those who pick on others. You don't have to hate one to love the other. God actually wants you to love both, but He wants your choices to look like His choices.

- -

I COULD MAKE CHOICES THAT ONLY HELP ME, GOD. BUT YOU WANT ME TO MAKE CHOICES THAT YOU WOULD MAKE. HELP ME THINK ABOUT THE THINGS YOU WOULD DO, THE THINGS YOU ASK, AND THEN MAKE THE RIGHT CHOICE.

MAKE YOUR CHOICE

Even if you suffer for doing what is right, you will be happy. Do not be afraid or troubled by what they may do to make it hard for you.
1 PETER 3:14

Every choice you'll ever make will have consequences, including the way people react to your choice and the way your choice makes you feel. It can even mean the trouble you get into or the honor you receive. Bad choices or good choices—you get to make them.

It may not seem fair, but you can make a good choice and be picked on for making it. You can be happy knowing you did the right thing. Even if other people make things hard for you, God is honored by your good choice.

Don't make your choices based on whether it makes your friends happy. Make your choices knowing that you've done what God wants you to do.

- -

YOU'RE MY FATHER, AND I WANT TO BRING HONOR TO YOU. I DON'T WANT TO MAKE MY CHOICES BASED ON WHAT I THINK MY FRIENDS WOULD DO, BUT BY THE WAY YOU TREAT ME. HELP ME SHARE THAT KIND OF LOVE WITH OTHERS.

IT'S HARD BEING YOUNG

Turn away from the sinful things young people want to do. Go after what is right. Have a desire for faith and love and peace. Do this with those who pray to God from a clean heart.
2 TIMOTHY 2:22

Being young can be hard. There are things you want to do, but you keep being told it's not the right time, not a good choice, or something you should never do. Sometimes you're told why you shouldn't do things, and other times you're just told no.

It's nice to understand why some choices are bad, but there are times you need to trust that doing something your friends want to do is off limits. Make right choices by holding tight to decisions that show your faith and offer God's love, and you'll be left with real peace.

For more help, find others who want to make the same kinds of choices. They can encourage your next right choice. Be a brave boy, follow God, and look for friendships that remind you to be brave.

- -

HELP ME STOP THINKING I NEED TO DO WHAT EVERYONE ELSE DOES, GOD. I WANT TO DO WHAT YOU WANT ME TO DO.

YOU WILL BE SATISFIED

"Those who are hungry and thirsty to be right with God are happy, because they will be filled."
MATTHEW 5:6

Have you ever missed lunch? You're pretty hungry when you get home, right? Have you ever been outside playing and had no water to drink? When you step inside, you're heading to the refrigerator, right? Keep that idea of hunger and thirst handy, because it's another good way to look at righteousness.

Get used to the taste of right living, and you may just want more. You will hunger and thirst for ways to please God. No, you won't actually taste righteousness, but you can see how making right choices leading to right living becomes a good way to please God. And when you please God, you will be satisfied.

This is a case of bravery meeting the goodness of God.

- -

MAKE ME HUNGRY AND THIRSTY TO PLEASE YOU, FATHER. HELP ME TO BE HAPPY WHEN I CHOOSE RIGHT LIVING OVER DOING WHAT I WANT TO DO. HELP ME TO BE SATISFIED KNOWING I'VE DONE THE RIGHT THING.

35

RIGHT. GOOD. FAIR.

*To do what is right and good and fair is more pleasing
to the Lord than gifts given on the altar in worship.*
PROVERBS 21:3

Does it ever seem as if you say you're sorry more than you're willing to make the right choice? That apology could be to your family, friends, or teachers. You might also find yourself apologizing to God. You may be in need of more forgiveness because you are making fewer right choices.

God is ready and willing to forgive anytime. But God also has something He likes even more. He would rather have you make good choices, do right things, and prove to be fair. He wants that more than an apology.

Why does this make God happy? It means you're growing up. You're paying attention to what He's teaching and you're obeying what He's asking you to do.

Right living, good choices, and being fair are three good ways to show that your new life is leading to new choices.

- -

YOU KNOW ALL THE BEST CHOICES, GOD. YOU CAN HELP ME
KNOW WHAT THEY ARE TOO. HELP ME PAY ATTENTION
AND CHOOSE TO LIVE RIGHT, GOOD, AND FAIR.

A DIFFERENT HOPE

Be happy in your hope. Do not give up when trouble comes. Do not let anything stop you from praying.
ROMANS 12:12

When you hear the word *hope*, you probably think of someone who wishes something good would happen. The Bible describes hope as putting your trust in God with the expectation of a good outcome.

As you read about hope over the next few days, remember the hope you read about here is not a wish but a belief that God is in control.

Hope can make you happy, because even when trouble comes, the ending is very different from the struggle you face. Use prayer to tell God all about what you're facing. Then tell Him you believe He can make things better. Remember: brave boys hope.

- -

TRUSTING THAT THE ENDING OF MY STORY WILL BE GOOD
IS THE BEST WAY FOR ME TO HOPE, FATHER. YOU'VE
PROMISED HELP. YOU SAID YOU LOVE ME. YOU SAID I
HAVE A FUTURE. HELP ME BELIEVE WHAT YOU'VE SAID.

HOPE GROWS

*Our hope comes from God. May He fill you with joy
and peace because of your trust in Him. May your
hope grow stronger by the power of the Holy Spirit.*
ROMANS 15:13

Hope comes from God because He has given you a reason to believe that what He says is what He'll do. He supplies joy and peace as you believe in the good things God has promised for those who love Him.

The reason hope goes beyond bravery is that hope requires bravery. It's a bit like faith. You don't always know when the good ending will show up, but you believe it is being delivered. This hope grows strong and beautiful because God's Spirit makes it grow.

When you have no hope, you have no trust. You think bad things will happen, and you feel very sad. Hope isn't just a good idea; it will improve your attitude, bring a smile, and help you feel certain about what comes next.

- -

I REALLY WANT YOUR SPIRIT TO HELP HOPE GROW, GOD. FROM
DEEP DOWN INSIDE, MAY I BELIEVE THAT YOU'RE STRONG
ENOUGH TO GIVE ME A FUTURE I CAN LOOK FORWARD TO.

FUTURE HOPE

We were saved with this hope ahead of us. Now hope means we are waiting for something we do not have. How can a man hope for something he already has? But if we hope for something we do not yet see, we must learn how to wait for it.
ROMANS 8:24–25

Why would you ever leave hope behind? Hope is something yet to come. It's something to look forward to, like Christmas morning. Hope believes there's something that belongs to you but a little waiting will be required. And waiting can be very hard.

When you get what you're waiting for, your hope is fulfilled. Years ago, people hoped for a Savior, and then Jesus arrived. Salvation is something people hoped for, and then Jesus offered it. Heaven is something to hope for, and the faithful Christ promises to come back and take you there. You can hope in God's promises. They always come true.

- -

YOU KEEP THE PROMISES YOU MAKE, FATHER. HELP ME TO REMEMBER THE PROMISES YOU HAVE ALREADY KEPT TO REMIND MYSELF THAT WHAT YOU HAVE FOR ME IN THE FUTURE IS GOING TO BE AMAZING.

39

DON'T GIVE UP

By not giving up, God's Word gives us strength and hope.
ROMANS 15:4

Sometimes giving up seems like an easy choice. It means no struggles, but it might also mean giving up a great outcome. When you give up, you let go of hope. Without hope you'll feel sad. When you feel sad, you become weak. When you're weak, you need hope.

When you feel sad and weak, you'll need the bravery God offers to trust that something good is coming from Him to you. That's why you don't give up. The choice to hold on can be tough because it means you'll need to be patient and brave and to believe in hope.

The best way to keep your hope alive is to keep reading the Bible. God says this is where strength and hope are found. It helps you when you want to give up and makes you less fearful and less confused. Hope makes it possible for you to hold on.

- -

YOU'RE GOD, AND EVERY BIT OF HOPE I HAVE COMES FROM YOU. HOLD ME UP, GIVE ME STRENGTH, AND HELP ME BELIEVE THE BEST IS YET TO COME.

YOUNG HOPE

For You are my hope, O Lord God.
You are my trust since I was young.
PSALM 71:5

If you are a brave *boy*, then you are also young. Developing hope at your age is just the right time to do it. Trusting God is a perfect thing to do. It lets you follow God for the longest amount of time. It helps you see how good God is. It's the right choice.

Following God now helps you avoid the most mistakes and spend the longest time learning, and it allows you to accept His love and forgiveness every day for the rest of your life.

Think about the joy you could experience, knowing that you chose to trust in God's perfect plan instead of waiting or, even worse, running away from God.

Remember, young brave boys hope because they trust.

- -

NOW IS A GOOD TIME TO HOPE IN YOU, FATHER. I CAN HOPE TODAY, TOMORROW, ALL YEAR, AND EVERY DAY OF MY LIFE. AND I DON'T HAVE TO WAIT. YOU GIVE ME ALL THE RIGHT REASONS TO TRUST.

HOPE ANSWERS

Always be ready to tell everyone who asks you why you believe as you do. Be gentle as you speak and show respect.
1 PETER 3:15

Why do you hope in God? Could you explain it? Have you ever thought about it, or does it just seem like the correct choice to make?

The choice to hope in God is a big one, and knowing what that means and why you should make that choice is important.

Hope in God is to be sure that He loves you, did everything to rescue you, and will come back to take you to heaven.

To have hope is to be sure that God is good, to believe that He saves, and to trust in His future. If that sounds like something you just read, you're right. Sometimes reading something twice can help you remember.

When you tell people about your hope, you don't need to be pushy or harsh. Some people are ready to hear about the hope you have.

- -

HELP ME TO REMEMBER WHY I HOPE IN YOU, GOD. THEN HELP ME TELL OTHERS HOW THEY CAN BE BRAVE ENOUGH TO HOPE IN YOU TOO.

THE LOVE LAW

[Jesus said,] "I give you a new Law. You are to love each other. You must love each other as I have loved you."
JOHN 13:34

Brave boys learn to follow a new law introduced by Jesus. That law is to love each other. Love your family, friends, and even those who aren't very nice to you. Love wants the best things to happen to others. Love doesn't try to hurt others or make them pay for mistakes. Love forgives and is kind.

This new law seems easy, but it can be very hard. Sometimes someone you're supposed to love can say or do something that hurts you. Making the choice to love them can seem impossible. Jesus can help. He will help. He does help.

Jesus showed the people who followed Him what they should expect love to look like. Then, once they saw love, Jesus asked them to take what they learned and love others the same way.

- -

THANK YOU FOR BEING WILLING TO TEACH ME HOW TO LOVE, FATHER. HELP ME TO BE WILLING TO LOVE PEOPLE THE WAY YOU LOVE THEM. MAYBE THEY CAN SEE YOU IN THE WAY I TREAT THEM.

THE HARD TO LOVE

We love Him because He loved us first. If a person says, "I love God," but hates his brother, he is a liar. If a person does not love his brother whom he has seen, how can he love God Whom he has not seen? We have these words from Him. If you love God, love your brother also.

1 JOHN 4:19–21

A good example is a pretty wonderful thing. If you follow a good example, then what you say will be the same message people discover when they see what you do. The Bible says it's possible to love people who are hard to love. Why? You've been loved by God when you were hard to love. You can't just say you love God if you won't love the people He created. The verse above says that if you say you love God and then refuse to love others, you're lying.

You can love the idea of loving God, but when you really love Him, it becomes possible to demonstrate love to people who might normally annoy you.

- -

I WANT TO LOVE YOU, GOD. AND HELP ME LOVE EVERYONE ELSE TOO.

44

THINK HARDER

Nothing should be done because of pride or thinking about yourself. Think of other people as more important than yourself.
PHILIPPIANS 2:3

If you only think of yourself when making a decision, then you haven't thought hard enough. God wants you to think bigger. Think about whether your choices might break God's rules. Think about whether your choices could hurt other people. Think about whether you might have a chance to help others.

People are important. That's true because God made them and He wants you to think of them as more important than yourself. That's a good decision, because if you always think of yourself first, you'll think you're the most important and you'll only make choices that make you happy and you won't make very many choices that help other people. God wants to use you to help people.

A brave boy like you loves others by helping when you can, being careful in what you say and do, and spending time thinking about what others might need.

- -

IT'S NOT VERY HARD TO THINK ABOUT WHAT I WANT, FATHER. HELP ME THINK ABOUT WHAT YOU WANT ME TO DO TO HELP OTHERS WHO MIGHT NEED HELP.

PEOPLE WILL NOTICE

*[Jesus said,] "If you love each other, all men
will know you are My followers."*
JOHN 13:35

There are times when a uniform helps other people to know you're a part of something bigger than yourself. You might have a badge, medal, or hat that tells people you're part of a team, club, or group. Most of the time you're proud to be a part, and you're glad other people recognize that the group means something to you.

For Christians, the badge you wear that causes people to notice is love. This one choice puts a spotlight on God. People will recognize God when they see His love in your choices. There should be something different about Christians. God's Word says that difference is the way we treat others. No revenge, no long-term anger, and no unkindness.

Love is a brave choice. Some people might not be as brave. They might still be frustrating, unkind, and willing to be a bully. That never has to be your choice.

- -

**I WANT PEOPLE TO NOTICE YOU WHEN THEY SEE MY
CHOICES, GOD. MAY OTHERS SEE YOU IN ME TODAY.**

TOGETHER

Love each other as Christian brothers.
Show respect for each other.
ROMANS 12:10

The brave choice to love sends a message to those who are Christians, and it also sends a message to those who don't follow God. It tells those who do follow God that you're willing to work together with them on God-sized projects. It tells those who don't follow that there's a difference in the lives of those who do follow. But no matter who you're around, you should respect them. Don't say mean things, listen when they speak, and admire the good things they do.

Love means you can work together, trust each other, and pray for each other. It's a picture of family that means something even when there are arguments and hurt feelings. God can forgive you, and you can forgive others. That's just what's needed among family and friends, and love never keeps others at a distance.

- -

LOVE IS MORE THAN JUST BEING NICE, FATHER. IT'S MORE THAN GOOD MANNERS. IT'S SOMETHING THAT STARTS IN THE HEART AND CHANGES ME AS I REACH OUT TO OTHERS WHO MIGHT JUST NEED A FRIEND LIKE YOU.

SOMETHING DIFFERENT THAN BRAGGING

Live and work without pride. Be gentle and kind. Do not be hard on others. Let love keep you from doing that.
EPHESIANS 4:2

Love doesn't decide that it's time to teach someone a lesson. Yes, you should learn, and people can learn from you. You might think that teaching someone a lesson means embarrassing someone who wronged you or means telling people things about that person that aren't true.

God can help you understand when you've made a wrong choice. God says it's normal for you to brag about the things you've done, but He wants you to do something different. He wants you to do your work without asking people to tell you what a great job you're doing. It's true, they might say something nice, but loving others means you don't have to force them to give you a compliment.

The love you can learn from God can put a stop to poor choices. That same love can keep you kind.

- -

KEEP ME FROM MAKING MY CHOICES ALL ABOUT ME, GOD. I CAN'T MAKE GOOD CHOICES WITHOUT YOUR HELP. THANK YOU FOR BEING WILLING TO HELP ME EVERY DAY.

MORE ROOM REQUIRED

Put out of your life all these things: bad feelings about other people, anger, temper, loud talk, bad talk which hurts other people, and bad feelings which hurt other people.
EPHESIANS 4:31

Do you have any bad feelings about other people? *Get rid of them.* Are you angry? *Send your anger away.* Is your temper out of control? *You'll need room for something else.* Do you yell at people? *Find your inside voice.* Do you hurt people by the way you talk? *Speak new words.* Do you remind people that you have bad feelings about something they've done? *Rediscover forgiveness.*

God can't find room in your life to do really good things when the room is taken up by hurt and anger. He can't work with you to help show kindness—often to people who might not deserve it. God can help you learn to leave hurt behind and find a new way to treat people He loves.

- -

I DON'T WANT TO MAKE ROOM IN MY LIFE FOR THINGS THAT MAKE IT HARDER TO HEAR YOU, FATHER. MAKE KINDNESS AND LOVE FIRST RESPONSES IN THE WAY I TREAT PEOPLE YOU LOVE.

DON'T MAKE THINGS WORSE

You must be kind to each other. Think of the other person. Forgive other people just as God forgave you because of Christ's death on the cross.
EPHESIANS 4:32

Brave boys are kind. When you get angry, stop and think. Don't talk and make things worse. Spend enough time to remember that God wants kindness first. That can change the direction of your choices, and it's a good change. It's the right change.

There are other people affected by your choices—*think of them.* There are people who will be mean—*forgive them.* You will have opportunities every day—*use them to be kind.* Make kindness a part of who you are.

Jesus endured more meanness than you ever will, and He made decisions to forgive the people who were mean. Now He asks you to forgive. He's not asking you to do something He's never done. He's asking you to be more like Him.

- -

FATHER, SOMETIMES I WANT TO SAY WORDS THAT TELL OTHERS HOW UPSET I AM FOR SOMETHING THEY DID. HELP ME TO REMEMBER THAT JESUS HAD EVERY REASON TO BE UPSET AND HE ASKED YOU TO FORGIVE PEOPLE LIKE ME.

ADJUSTED TREATMENT

"Do for other people whatever you would like to have them do for you."
MATTHEW 7:12

You've probably heard of the Golden Rule. Jesus didn't call it that. He had kindness on His mind, but the verse above wasn't called the Golden Rule until two men named it in 1604. Charles Gibbon and Thomas Jackson helped brave boys remember that the rule of kindness, treating people fairly and choosing honesty, is important to God.

This rule is something anyone can follow—just treat others the way you want to be treated. If you want kindness, then give kindness. If you want friendship, then be a friend. The opposite is also true. Say mean things to someone else, and you'll probably hear them say mean things about you. Laugh when someone has been embarrassed, and they will laugh at you.

If you want to do your part in changing the world, then adjust how you treat other people.

- -

I'M NOT ALWAYS TREATED FAIRLY, AND I DON'T ALWAYS TREAT OTHERS THE WAY I WANT TO BE TREATED, FATHER. CHANGE MY MIND, MY HEART, AND MY WORDS SO I CAN FOLLOW YOUR RULE OF KINDNESS.

NO MORE HIDE AND KEEP

There is one who is free in giving, and yet he grows richer. And there is one who keeps what he should give, but he ends up needing more.
PROVERBS 11:24

Do you have a heart that keeps more than it gives, hides more than it shares, and takes more than it needs? The verse above says that when you keep what you should share, you somehow end up with less than you need. But if you give, you will somehow have more.

Generosity and kindness are important to God. When you think, *That's mine, and no one can have it*, you might just lose more than you ever thought you'd save.

To see someone hurting or needing help and making the choice not to help makes you poor in spirit, in friendships, and in kindness. There are things you can never earn. They are gifts from God that are worth sharing. And you can keep them.

- -

I WANT TO REMEMBER THAT SOME OF YOUR BEST GIFTS ARE MINE TO SHARE, FATHER. WHEN I KEEP THEM TO MYSELF, I LOSE SOME OF THE WONDER OF YOUR GOODNESS.

MORE THAN YOU STARTED WITH

The man who gives much will have much, and he who helps others will be helped himself.
PROVERBS 11:25

Your choices are like a field, and you can plant things like kindness, love, and compassion. The harvest will be worth more than it took to plant those seeds. There are other crops you could plant, and the harvest for those crops will be pretty good too. But what if you choose to plant rudeness, distrust, and bullying? You'll have a harvest that no one wants to see.

Kindness grows where it's planted. It's a beautiful crop, and people like what they see. But bullying also grows where it's planted. It's a crop no one wants, but it will keep growing unless it's pulled up by the roots.

Give and help. That's when you will receive and be helped. When you plant good seeds, you'll always end up with more than you started with.

- -

FATHER, THANK YOU FOR SHOWING ME THAT WHATEVER KINDS OF SEEDS I PLANT GIVE AN INCREASE. GOOD CHOICES LEAD TO MORE GOOD, AND BAD CHOICES HURT PEOPLE.

A DISPLAY OF KINDNESS

*"[God] is kind to those who are not thankful
and to those who are full of sin."*
LUKE 6:35

Does God want you to be kind? Yes. It seems like a silly question. You know that God wants brave boys to be kind. But what if you're not kind—then what? God shows kindness when you won't. When you can't say thank you and when you often break God's laws, He will still show kindness to you.

If God decided not to be kind, how would you know what kindness looks like? What example would you have? Accept His kindness, and then be kind to others. Be thankful and find more things to be thankful for.

When you want to be more than brave, take kindness with you. It's brave to bring something with you that no one expects. On the other hand, fear wants you to fight back. Fear hurts other people.

- -

IT'S NOT MY JOB TO PUNISH ANYONE, GOD. YOU ASK ME TO
LOVE OTHERS AND SHOW KINDNESS. KEEP ME FROM TRYING
TO MAKE PEOPLE PAY BY KEEPING KINDNESS TO MYSELF.

LOYAL AND BRAVE

Watch and keep awake! Stand true to the Lord.
Keep on acting like men and be strong.
1 CORINTHIANS 16:13

Taking a spiritual nap can be dangerous because God's enemy Satan hates you. He loves it when you aren't paying attention to God. He would love to help you think of anything else. He even wants you to think of God as your enemy. That's why you must stand up, stand true, and stand strong. That's why you need to be loyal.

You grow up a little more every time you give God first place. That kind of loyalty is the same kind of loyalty God has for you. He stays with you, walks with you, and guides when you don't know where to go. Think of all the ways you can walk with God and be both loyal and brave.

- -

MY LOYALTY TO YOU IS WHAT YOU WANT, FATHER. HELP ME NEVER TO BE ASHAMED TO SAY THAT I FOLLOW YOU. HELP ME TO PAY ATTENTION TO YOUR INSTRUCTIONS FOR AN AMAZING LIFE.

MORE THAN BITS AND PIECES

Do not let kindness and truth leave you. Tie them around your neck. Write them upon your heart.
PROVERBS 3:3

Be loyal to God. Be loyal to His message. Don't leave bits and pieces of His wisdom lying around like empty candy wrappers you no longer need. His teachings are important for you to remember and important for you to share. Keep them close enough that you will always be reminded. Write them on your heart so you won't forget.

There is no loyalty in choosing only the parts of God's Word you want to believe. If you say you follow but don't do what God asks, are you really following?

Hold tight to kindness. Grip truth and never let it go. Know for sure that when you kindly speak the truth, God can use your obedience to help someone see Him and understand that He loves them.

LOYALTY TO YOUR WISDOM ISN'T JUST A GOOD IDEA, FATHER; IT'S HOW ANYONE CAN HAVE AN ABUNDANT LIFE. IT'S HOW I CAN HAVE AN ABUNDANT LIFE. I WANT YOUR HELP. KEEP ME MAKING THE CHOICE TO FOLLOW.

LOVE IS LOYAL

Love takes everything that comes without giving up. Love believes all things. Love hopes for all things. Love keeps on in all things.
1 CORINTHIANS 13:7

Love is loyalty. God said that love doesn't give up, believes the best, hopes in God's plan, and keeps going when it would be easier to stop.

Maybe you've never thought of love as being loyal, but love stands with people when others leave, and *that* is loyalty. Jesus stands with you when others walk away; His love is loyal.

When you take all you've learned about being brave, then choose to love, you will understand that you both give and receive loyalty. You need the loyalty of God, and then as you choose to be loyal to Him, you will grow in the truth that God's way—life in Christ—is the way to a full life.

Yes, it may seem easier to stop, but keep following God's way to life.

- -

I DON'T ALWAYS THINK OF LOYALTY WHEN I THINK OF LOVE, FATHER. HELP ME TO REMEMBER THAT LOVE IS A LOYAL CHOICE. IT'S THE WAY YOU LOVE ME AND IT'S THE WAY I CAN SAY, "I LOVE YOU" WITH MY WORDS AND ACTIONS.

FAITHFUL WITHOUT APPLAUSE

Many men tell about their own loving-kindness and good ways but who can find a faithful man?
PROVERBS 20:6

If a guest speaker comes to your school, someone will introduce them. You're told about many good things they've done. You'll hear about their accomplishments. You'll learn that they've earned awards. Then they will speak, and you might wonder if you'll ever be as important.

Loyalty to God is *faithfulness without applause*. It's helping without needing an award. It's giving without thinking someone should give to you. You obey God, show generosity, and find ways to be kind. You can do this knowing that God is paying attention.

You don't need a front-page news story to be loyal. Not everyone who tells others about all they have done is actually loyal. Some just want to be recognized.

- -

YOU ARE GOD, AND YOU ARE LOYAL. I FOLLOW, AND I WANT TO BE THOUGHT OF AS FAITHFUL. I WON'T ALWAYS GET IT RIGHT. I MIGHT WANT PEOPLE TO NOTICE THE GOOD THINGS I DO. HELP ME TO BE LOYAL TO YOU. MAY I REMEMBER THAT YOUR OPINION IS WHAT'S MOST IMPORTANT.

TRUST GUARANTEE?

Peter said to [Jesus], "Even if I have to die with
You, I will never say I do not know You."
MATTHEW 26:35

When you're disloyal, you can be thought of as someone who betrays, someone who is unfaithful, or someone who abandons. These characteristics would never describe God, but in today's verse they do describe one disciple.

Peter guaranteed his faithfulness to Jesus. But Jesus kindly spoke the truth. He told Peter that he would say he didn't know Jesus—not once or even twice, but three times in the same night.

Peter wanted to be loyal. He thought he could be. Yet when strangers recognized Peter as someone who followed Jesus, that was the moment Peter told each person that he didn't even know who Jesus was. Isn't it amazing that God hasn't and won't deny that you're part of His family when you agree to be rescued?

- -

YOUR EXAMPLE IS SO IMPORTANT, FATHER. I COULD NEVER REALLY UNDERSTAND THE VALUE OF LOYALTY IF I HADN'T SEEN HOW LOYAL YOU ARE TO ME. I MAY NOT BE ABLE TO GUARANTEE LOYALTY, BUT BY THE HELP OF YOUR HOLY SPIRIT IN ME, I WILL DO MY BEST TO STAY TRUE TO YOU.

FAITHFUL IS HIS NAME

*If we have no faith, He will still be faithful
for He cannot go against what He is.*
2 TIMOTHY 2:13

You've made the wrong choice, broken God's law, and sinned. Everyone has. Everyone will. Sin keeps a distance between you and God. You were not faithful. That may be hard to read, but God says it's the truth. The good news is that God *is* faithful when you're not. He can't become unfaithful because *Faithful* is one of His names. He can't be something He's not. That's why you won't find Him breaking His own law, being disloyal, and deciding He no longer wants to be faithful.

A brave boy like you can learn that faithfulness can start all over again when you ask God to help you make faithful choices. Forgiveness starts things fresh and new.

If God waited for you to be 100 percent faithful before He could help, then help wouldn't come. He loves you. He's loyal. He's faithful.

- -

I LOVE READING GOOD NEWS, GOD. YOUR FAITHFULNESS TO ME IS REALLY GOOD NEWS. HELP ME TO REMEMBER THAT YOU WILL ALWAYS BE FAITHFUL, LOYAL, AND KIND. WITH YOUR HELP, I CAN LEARN.

COMPARISONS

Everyone should look at himself and see how he does his own work. Then he can be happy in what he has done. He should not compare himself with his neighbor.

GALATIANS 6:4

Today's verse tells you that you have a responsibility to examine yourself and what you do. Earlier in this book, you've read about some areas in which you are responsible to do good, like loving others, forgiving those who hurt you, and being kind even when someone doesn't seem to deserve kindness. But these responsibilities aren't part of a contest to see who is better, so you shouldn't compare yourself to anyone else. If you want to compete, you should compete against yourself. Do better this time than last. Follow more faithfully, lovingly, and in awe of God's forgiveness.

Even if the first thing you ever do as a Christian is to follow, then you have the responsibility to move to the place where God leads you. So watch what you do, do your work well, and be happy when you finish your work.

- -

CHEERING OTHER CHRISTIANS ON IN THEIR WALK WITH YOU IS SOMETHING I CAN DO, FATHER. HELP ME ONLY COMPARE WHAT I DID TODAY WITH WHAT I DID YESTERDAY.

NOT THE SAME JOB

The one who plants and the one who waters are
alike. Each one will receive his own reward.
1 CORINTHIANS 3:8

What sort of responsibilities do you have around the house? Things like making your bed, taking out the trash, or feeding the dog? Other people in your house also have responsibilities, but they aren't the same as yours. Someone might make a meal. Someone else might clean it up. Someone might mow the lawn. Someone else might do the laundry. When everyone works, a lot gets done. That's what the verse above is trying to help you learn. Not every Christian does the exact same thing for Jesus, but when you pay attention to what you need to do, then others can pay attention to what they are supposed to do. In the end, Jesus is pleased with the work you do and the work they did.

- -

HELP ME PAY ATTENTION TO THE THINGS I'M RESPONSIBLE FOR, GOD. HELP ME CHEER OTHERS WHO ARE DOING THE SAME THING. I DON'T NEED TO DO BETTER THAN OTHERS, MAYBE JUST BETTER THAN I'VE DONE THINGS BEFORE.

FAITHFUL AND HONEST

"He that is faithful with little things is faithful with big things also. He that is not honest with little things is not honest with big things."
LUKE 16:10

When you're given a job to do in your home, you can either do it or you can make excuses. Not doing what you were asked to do probably means you won't be asked to help with bigger jobs. Many kids get excited when their mom or dad trust them enough to ask them for help, but if they don't finish their jobs, they might not be trusted to help for a while.

You want to do big things, right? Well, the good news is that big things start with doing small things well. When you're honest in small things, you will be more likely to be honest in big things. Big things always start with doing small things to the best of your ability.

- -

I WANT TO BE FAITHFUL, FATHER. HELP ME TO BE HONEST. ADD SOME OBEDIENCE AND COMPASSION. I WANT TO START SMALL SO I CAN BE READY WHEN YOU HAVE BIGGER THINGS FOR ME TO DO.

CURRENT CHORE CHART

Whatever work you do, do it with all your heart.
Do it for the Lord and not for men.
COLOSSIANS 3:23

Brave boys want to get things done. They don't want to leave things half-finished. They know that what they need to do isn't just a chore; it's the chance to show God that they are thankful. They clean, pick up, and lend a hand, knowing that doing so pleases God.

Work hard, remembering that you're working for God. The things you do for your family are more than just chores; they are opportunities to show that you are learning more about the One who has been faithful in doing the most work in the best possible way. That is exactly what God has done and is doing for you.

- -

FATHER, HELP ME TO HAVE A GOOD ATTITUDE ABOUT THE WORK I AM ASKED TO DO. DOING MY BEST IS A WAY FOR ME TO SHOW THAT I LOVE YOU AND AM THANKFUL FOR WHAT YOU HAVE DONE AND ARE DOING FOR ME.

GIVE. HELP. SHARE.

*Go to the ant, O lazy person. Watch and
think about her ways, and be wise.*
PROVERBS 6:6

You can take and never give. You can be helped and never help. You can even have and never share. None are great options. Make a better choice.

God wants you to think about how the ant does things. If you think the only things ants do are bite and steal picnic food, then you don't see how hard they work. They store up food for winter, and they work as a team. The Bible says you're wise if you pay attention to the ant. God must want you to do more than take and keep.

Remember, ants give. They help. They share. All are great options—for the ant and for you too.

- -

YOU GIVE, HELP, AND SHARE, FATHER. I EXPECT THAT FROM YOU. BUT YOU EXPECT THAT YOUR FAMILY WILL DO THE SAME. I SHOULD LOVE OTHERS AND HELP BECAUSE I HAVE BEEN HELPED. GIVE ME THE CHANCE, THE HEART, AND THE COURAGE TO HELP WHEN HELP IS NEEDED.

GOD'S GROWTH GUIDE

When I was a child, I spoke like a child. I thought like a child. I understood like a child. Now I am a man. I do not act like a child anymore.

1 CORINTHIANS 13:11

When you were three years old, you walked, talked, and acted like you were three years old. When you were eight, everything about you was different than when you were three. When you're twenty-one, that will be entirely different than today. You will think differently and understand differently. You will even work differently.

Wouldn't it be strange to become a man and still act like you're three? The change may be slow, but as you learn and grow and as you work and become a responsible young man, you and everyone around you will notice a difference.

I'LL HAVE TO BE BRAVE IF I'M GOING TO GROW, GOD. IT'S EASY TO BE WHO I AM TODAY, BUT TO THINK OF THE DAY I'LL BE A MAN SEEMS A LITTLE FRIGHTENING. HELP ME GET THERE AND TO BE COURAGEOUS ENOUGH TO FOLLOW YOU TO MY FUTURE.

DISHONESTY'S JOURNEY

The Lord hates lying lips, but those who
speak the truth are His joy.
PROVERBS 12:22

Your mouth creates words that started their journey in your mind and heart. By the time those words get to your lips, you have made a choice. You've decided that your words will either be truthful or will lie. In the past when you've lied, it was no accident. You probably thought about what you would say if you were asked. You may have made the choice just before you spoke, but it was still a choice you made.

God would love to see dishonesty go away. It allows people to hear something that's untrue but which they believe to be true. They can then take what they think is true and share it, making the dishonest statement available everywhere. No wonder so many people are confused. Speak the truth and know that you've given God joy.

- -

I NEED TO CHOOSE MY WORDS CAREFULLY, FATHER. HELP ME LOVE PEOPLE ENOUGH THAT I WILL CHOOSE WORDS THAT ARE TRUE AND HELPFUL. HELP ME DECIDE TO BE HONEST BEFORE I SPEAK. I WANT TO BE THAT BRAVE.

FROM TRUST TO TRUTH

"You will know the truth and the truth will make you free."
JOHN 8:32

Truth is extremely important to God. Have you ever wondered why? Think about how much trust you'd be willing to give to God if He told you things that were untrue or if He made promises He had no intention of keeping. You follow God because He speaks truth and He leads perfectly. His truth leads to freedom you need.

God isn't dishonest or dishonorable. He doesn't distort or deceive. God defines truth, and you can discover it in the Bible.

Being a brave boy means reading truth, believing truth, and sharing truth. This is honesty first, last, and above all.

Learn truth, and you will be free to share truth. Turn your back on truth, and you'll be unable to tell others about the love and power that can change their lives.

- -

KNOWING THAT YOU ARE ENTIRELY TRUTHFUL HELPS ME TRUST YOU, GOD. I NEED TO HAVE FAITH IN YOU, BECAUSE WHEN I DON'T, I CAN THINK YOU'RE TRYING TO DECEIVE ME. BUT YOU NEVER HAVE—AND YOU WON'T BEGIN TODAY.

HE HATES THE CHOICE

The Lord hates. . .a lying tongue, and. . .
a person who tells lies about someone else.
PROVERBS 6:16–17, 19

God hates lying. It's not helpful, and it can hurt other people. God doesn't hate people, but He does hate the choice that separates people. That's what lies do. Lies can even keep you away from God.

Honest words might also make someone upset or unhappy, but the end result of honest words is helping someone see where they went wrong, stop making unwise choices, and move in a better direction. Honesty should bring with it kindness, love, and concern.

God is trustworthy, and He wants His family to be considered trustworthy too. He wants what you think, say, and do to be completely honest. People are more willing to trust someone who is honest and really cares about them.

- -

IT SOMETIMES SEEMS EASIER TO LIE THAN TO TELL THE TRUTH, FATHER. HELP ME FIND A WAY TO TELL THE TRUTH AND THEN HELP OTHERS UNDERSTAND THAT I REALLY DO CARE ABOUT THEM BECAUSE YOU CARE ABOUT ME.

NEVER IGNORED OR OVERLOOKED

*Do not lie to each other. You have put
out of your life your old ways.*
COLOSSIANS 3:9

When you break a God law and try to hide what you've done, you're being dishonest with yourself. God knows, and He won't ignore, overlook, or pretend you didn't do what you actually did. He wants you to be honest, but when you fail you need to seek forgiveness. Lying means that there will come a point when you'll need to be honest, and it's always harder when you wait.

When you lie to someone, you're breaking a God law and need to seek forgiveness from God and the person you lied to. Before you followed Jesus Christ, you may have lied, but now that you are serving Him, lying must stop.

Brave boys learn that there's a responsibility to be honest, truthful, and kind. This is what God wants, and it's a choice you should take seriously.

- -

CHANGE MY HEART ABOUT HONESTY, GOD. HELP ME
STOP PRETENDING I'M HONEST. I REALLY WANT TO BE
HONEST. MAY MY WORDS HONOR YOU AND ALLOW
OTHER PEOPLE TO SEE THAT I FOLLOW YOUR EXAMPLE.

GUILT-FREE

*"I always try to live so my own heart tells me
I am not guilty before God or man."*
ACTS 24:16

God has given you the honor of knowing what He wants. He doesn't leave you guessing. Once you learn God's laws and know that He wants you to love instead of hate, today's verse might begin to make sense.

Know what God says and live in a way that your own heart says, *Not guilty.*

If you don't know what God wants, then it's pretty hard to know if you've made a good choice. The good news is that God gives you His Spirit who can help you learn and then help you make the best choices.

So, today you get to decide. Will you learn? Will you choose to live the life of a follower who knows what God wants and then does what He asks? God can help you honestly follow.

- -

WHEN I FOLLOW, HELP ME LEARN WHAT THAT MEANS, FATHER. HELP ME TO BE FAITHFUL AND HONEST IN READING THE BIBLE SO I CAN KNOW WHAT YOU WANT. WHEN I KNOW WHAT TO DO, WOULD YOU HELP ME OBEY?

RIGHT STANDING BRINGS LIFE

You get what is coming to you when you sin. It is death! But God's free gift is life that lasts forever. It is given to us by our Lord Jesus Christ.

ROMANS 6:23

You want to be right with God, but what does that mean? When you understand that Jesus has chosen you and you give your life to Him, the sacrifice of His life on the cross takes away your sin. *That's forgiveness.* Jesus reminds God that He paid the price for every moment you're not right with Him.

Being right with God will always mean seeking forgiveness, but it will also encourage truthfulness and inspire love. Think for a moment about all the things God has done for you in the past and then of the future He has waiting for you. When you acknowledge His faithfulness in the past, you can be brave and trust Him with your future—life that lasts forever.

- -

YOU'RE AN AMAZING GOD. THANKING YOU IS A SMALL GIFT COMPARED TO THE MANY GIFTS YOU GIVE TO ME—ESPECIALLY LIFE THAT LASTS FOREVER. HELP ME TO BE HONEST WITH OTHERS ABOUT HOW GOOD YOU ARE, AND THEN HELP ME LIVE LIKE I'M GRATEFUL.

THE RIGHT THING

If you know what is right to do but you do not do it, you sin.
JAMES 4:17

Knowing the right thing to do is important. Doing the right thing is obedience. Admitting when you have not done the right thing is acknowledging your sin. Today's verse is a good test for the choices you make. The more you learn from God, the more you can recognize the value of your choices. You can begin to recognize when the choice you've made requires a visit with God so you can admit that He was right and that you made the wrong choice.

Knowing the right thing to do isn't enough. God wants you to *do* the right thing. Look around you to see what you can do to help someone else in Jesus' name. Don't ignore the need. If you don't help, who will?

- -

FATHER, I DON'T WANT TO MISS OPPORTUNITIES TO DO THE RIGHT THING. HELP ME RECOGNIZE WHEN I'VE BLOWN IT, SEEK FORGIVENESS, LEARN FROM MY MISTAKES, AND THEN ASK FOR YOUR HELP TO MAKE A BETTER CHOICE NEXT TIME.

WHAT NEEDS TO BE DONE

"I do want to finish the work the Lord Jesus gave me to do.
My work is to preach the Good News of God's loving-favor."
ACTS 20:24

Have you ever started a puzzle? You're excited about the project. Maybe you get all the straight pieces put together, but then it gets hard. It isn't long before all the pieces sort of look alike and you find yourself giving up. You put the pieces back in the box, and you're convinced you'll never put another puzzle together again.

You can make that decision, and no one will think much about it because puzzles can be hard. But God has given you something to do, and you need to take initiative to do it. You need to do what needs to be done. When you want to do the work, God wants to help you get it done. People need to know about Jesus, and as long as you're alive there will be people who need to hear about Jesus from you.

- -

MAKE ME BRAVE ENOUGH TO TELL PEOPLE ABOUT YOU,
GOD. THEY NEED TO HEAR IT. I NEED TO SAY IT.

HAVE WISE FRIENDS

He who walks with wise men will be wise, but the
one who walks with fools will be destroyed.
PROVERBS 13:20

Did you know that you can choose the friends you want to spend time with? You can do what needs to be done to make sure you are friends with people who will encourage you to follow God. Today's verse says it's wise to have wise friends and it's a bad choice to spend too much time with people who think it's silly to follow God.

When you don't take initiative in your friendships, you're not being brave. Being brave means you'll do everything you can to find friends who follow God. You may have to get out of your comfort zone and be bold about talking to other people about your relationship with Jesus. When you do, you may be surprised to find others who know Him and still others who would like to know Him—and your circle of friends will grow.

- -

YOU WANT ME TO BE WISE, FATHER. I CAN MAKE FOOLISH
CHOICES WITHOUT ANY HELP, BUT MAKING GOOD ONES MEANS
I WILL NEED YOUR HELP AND THE HELP OF WISE FRIENDS.
GUIDE ME IN FINDING AND MAKING THOSE FRIENDS.

RESPONDING TO BULLIES

*A gentle answer turns away anger, but
a sharp word causes anger.*
PROVERBS 15:1

Imagine that someone comes up to you and says something mean. You think of them as a bully because they've also been saying mean things to people you know and care about. What do you do? What do you want to do?

If you said something like, "I'd tell them what I really think," then your answer is a lot like the way most people would answer, but it's not the way God wants you to respond.

If Jesus had responded that way, He would have responded to the bullies He met with the answer of a bully. Instead, He chose to forgive, and He rarely chose anger. Jesus knew that when someone speaks angry words, a gentle answer will stop anger. When there's no one to argue with, then there's no reason to be angry. Do what needs to be done to reduce anger in other people.

- -

IT'S HARD NOT TO GET ANGRY WHEN SOMEONE IS MEAN, GOD.
HELP ME LEARN WHY IT'S SO IMPORTANT TO BE BRAVE ENOUGH
TO BE KIND WHEN THAT'S NOT WHAT I HEAR IN OTHERS.

LET THEM SEE JESUS

"Let your light shine in front of men. Then they will see the good things you do and will honor your Father Who is in heaven."
MATTHEW 5:16

You can't shine your light if you refuse to let people see it. That's not just the light of a good personality, but the light of something different that people notice about you—the light of Jesus.

Take the initiative to show people the difference Jesus makes in your life. Why wouldn't you want them to see the impressive things He's done in your life? Why wouldn't you want them to honor the God who can change human hearts, personal failings, and the way people think?

When Jesus came, He spent His time talking about the message He came to share. He wasn't embarrassed to share it. He knew the value of the message, so He taught it.

If people don't see Jesus in you, what are they seeing?

- -

YOU AREN'T JUST THE GREATEST HELPER, FATHER, YOU'RE THE ONE WHO CHANGED MY LIFE WITH THE BEST NEWS I'VE EVER HEARD. HELP ME TO BE BRAVE ENOUGH TO PUT A SPOTLIGHT ON YOUR LOVE.

THE RESCUING CREATOR

*[Jesus] made all things. Nothing was
made without Him making it.*

JOHN 1:3

Jesus isn't just the One who rescues people from sin; He's also the great Creator. Everything on earth was made by Him. He took the initiative to give you a planet to live on, people to care about you, and a future that exists beyond His creation and because of His rescue.

Jesus did what needed to be done to start life, keep life going, and rescue life. He made all things that people make things from. Nothing would exist if He hadn't done that.

He made this decision so you could make decisions that either bring you closer to Him or move you further away from Him. He doesn't make you love Him, but He has given brave boys like you every reason to make that incredible choice.

- -

IT'S AMAZING TO THINK OF ALL THAT JESUS HAS DONE, FATHER. HE'S MORE THAN A NICE IDEA. HE'S MORE IMPRESSIVE THAN MY GREATEST AWARD. HE GAVE ME LIFE AND THEN A REASON TO LIVE IT. THAT'S INITIATIVE, AND I'M ALIVE AND I'M GRATEFUL.

BRAVERY—HOPE—JOY

The hope of those who are right with God is joy,
but the hope of the sinful comes to nothing.
PROVERBS 10:28

Bravery is how you respond when hard days show up. Hope is what you experience when you know God's plan is good and He won't leave you to figure things out on your own. Brave boys need hope, and hope brings joy. That's something much better than happiness, because you can have joy even when life hands you a bad day.

Joy remembers that God is bigger than your bad day and that the future God plans for you is so much better than your worst moment. Like hope, joy trusts that God's better day will make bad days totally forgettable. Hope will always bring brave boys joy.

Those who don't have that hope and aren't that brave will not have joy. Their best plans are not God's plans. Their best dreams cannot compare to God's. Their choices will disappoint.

- -

HELP ME TO REMEMBER THAT YOU ARE WHERE I FIND JOY, FATHER. IT'S EASY TO FEEL SAD WHEN I THINK I NEED TO BE HAPPY, BUT YOU WANT ME TO FIND JOY BECAUSE IT'S YOUR GIFT THAT NEVER LEAVES.

THE WAY OF LIFE

*You will show me the way of life. Being
with You is to be full of joy.*
PSALM 16:11

Some people think you need to have more, do more, and take more to have the best life. God wants you to know that has never been the real way of life. The things you have or think you need have nothing to do with the things God knows are important.

God actually wants you to trade the way you think life should be and let Him change your opinion. His life plan is a friendship that never leaves or forsakes. He's there in the hardest moments on the worst days. He'll never suggest you need stuff more than you need Him. Why? Well, stuff might bring happiness, but it never lasts too long. A friendship with God is forever, and it brings joy that never ends.

Brave boys pay attention to what God's way of life looks like.

- -

**JUST BECAUSE I MIGHT THINK SOMETHING IS RIGHT,
IT WILL NEVER BE RIGHT IF YOU SAY IT'S WRONG,
GOD. THERE'S JOY IN HAVING YOU AS A FRIEND.**

MORE IMPORTANT

For the holy nation of God is not food and drink. It is being right with God. It is peace and joy given by the Holy Spirit.
ROMANS 14:17

Eating food and drinking fluids keeps you alive, but they're not why you live. God has an important future, and it's possible to get so caught up caring about hunger and thirst that you can't remember the real reason for living.

Life is being obedient to God. The gift of this kind of life is peace and joy. It's not stress, anger, or what you want for supper. God wants you to be able to eat and drink, but He wants you to think about what's *more* important.

Why do you think God would want you to experience peace more than looking at a menu? Why might God want you to have joy more than swallowing your favorite drink?

- -

SOMETIMES I CAN GET THINGS BACKWARD, FATHER. I CAN FORGET ABOUT WHAT'S IMPORTANT TO YOU AND REPLACE IT WITH THINGS I LIKE. HELP ME TO REMEMBER THAT YOUR PEACE AND JOY ARE GIFTS THAT I CAN NEVER BUY.

WHAT HE DOES TODAY

This is the day that the Lord has made. Let us be full of joy and be glad in it.

PSALM 118:24

God made yesterday, but what you're experiencing right now is called today, and God made that too. This is a day that is unlike any other in history. And because you don't have to remember what it was like or wonder what it will be, you can just enjoy today. You can express joy because what you're experiencing is linked to God's plan for your life. You can be happy too, because what you're experiencing might just bring fun to your day.

The bravery found in joy has a lot to do with walking with God. He made today and is here today, and He's not going to walk away today. Remember His goodness found in the past, but walk with Him today. Look forward to His future, but pay attention to what He does today. He made it to bring you joy. It sounds like today could be a pretty wonderful day.

- -

EVERY DAY IS A NEW ADVENTURE, GOD. I CAN HAVE YOUR JOY BY PAYING ATTENTION TO THE PLACE YOU'RE TAKING ME TODAY.

CHASING JOY

*A glad heart is good medicine, but a
broken spirit dries up the bones.*
PROVERBS 17:22

If you've ever wondered why you should chase after joy, it has everything to do with what you could chase. God's Word calls joy a very good medicine. If joy is trusting God's plan, then the opposite is not trusting, and that leads to a broken spirit. And when your spirit is broken, you are left in a place that is dry, empty, and less meaningful.

See? Chase joy. When you find it, you'll find life, refreshment, and fulfillment. Maybe this verse was placed in the Bible so you could compare the difference joy can make. Knowing this difference is important because it gives you all the information you need to choose joy. That kind of joy brings life to a spirit that's been dry and empty too long. *Finding joy is finding life.*

- -

THERE ARE TIMES I HAVEN'T THOUGHT ENOUGH ABOUT THE GOOD THINGS YOU OFFER, FATHER. BRING MY HEART, MIND, AND SPIRIT TOGETHER SO I CAN RECOGNIZE JOY AND BEGIN THE CHASE. HELP ME CATCH THE REASONS FOR JOY AND USE THAT JOY AS YOUR GOOD MEDICINE.

WHAT GOD WANTS

Be full of joy all the time. Never stop praying. In everything give thanks. This is what God wants you to do.
1 THESSALONIANS 5:16–18

You might think it's hard to know what God wants you to do. Today you can learn about three different things that mean something to Him. How can you know? The verse above answers the question with no need for guessing, "This is what God wants you to do."

"Be full of joy all the time." Make the full-time choice to believe God has a better day coming.

"Never stop praying." Keep talking to God. He'll keep listening to you and answering you.

"In everything give thanks." You can thank God for everything because God can bring good from even bad experiences.

Why do you think these three things are important to God? Why should they be important to you? Why do you think you should choose joy and never stop?

- -

BECAUSE I WANT TO DO WHAT YOU WANT ME TO DO,
GOD, I THANK YOU FOR HELPING ME UNDERSTAND THAT
JOY, PRAYER, AND THANKSGIVING ARE IMPORTANT
TO YOU. MAKE THEM IMPORTANT TO ME.

THE AUTHOR

We know that God makes all things work
together for the good of those who love Him
and are chosen to be a part of His plan.
ROMANS 8:28

Earlier you read that God can cause good to come from bad situations. Today you'll learn that He does this for the rescued. When you love God and follow His plan, He can take bad things and rewrite the story with a surprise ending.

You can be satisfied leaving your story in the hands of a God who is called the Author (see Hebrews 12:2). Your story is very different from any other, and God can take painful mistakes, physical hurt, and the way people have treated you and somehow use His Author's pen to make it a story worth telling. When you trust God, you are content, or satisfied. That can be part of any brave boy's story.

- -

SOMETIMES THINGS THAT HAPPEN TO ME ARE CONFUSING, FATHER. I DON'T WANT TO STRUGGLE, BUT THEN I DO. HELP ME TRUST THAT AS I FOLLOW YOU, PEOPLE WILL SEE MORE THAN STRUGGLE. HELP THEM SEE YOU WORKING ON MY LIFE STORY.

WISDOM SATISFIED

Do not let me be poor or rich. Feed me with the food that I need. Then I will not be afraid that I will be full and turn my back against You and say, "Who is the Lord?" And I will not be afraid that I will be poor and steal, and bring shame on the name of my God.
PROVERBS 30:8–9

Agur, the man who wrote this parable, said there were problems with being poor. He said there were problems with being rich. Being poor might cause him to steal. Being rich might cause him to turn away from God. He wanted just enough from God to keep trusting.

Satisfaction trusts that God knows what to provide even when it's less or more than you want. God knows what you need. That also means that He knows what you don't need. Find joy in accepting what God gives. He takes care of you as you learn from Him.

- -

I DON'T WANT TO BE RESTLESS, THINKING YOU SHOULD GIVE ME MORE THAN I HAVE, GOD. GIVE ME WHAT I NEED AND HELP ME TO BE SATISFIED.

MORE ALIVE

A heart that has peace is life to the body, but wrong desires are like the wasting away of the bones.
PROVERBS 14:30

You can throw away gifts God meant for you to use to help others. You can be helpful, or you can be selfish. The choices you make might make sense to you, but if they don't make sense to God, then the choice you make is described as "the wasting away of the bones." This means the impact of your life becomes a little smaller.

When you're satisfied doing what God wants you to do, you find peace and feel more alive. Contentment comes with doing just what you were created to do.

God created a satisfaction path for you to follow. By staying on the path, you get to the adventure sooner. When you walk off the path to check something out, you waste time getting to God's good plan for you.

- -

I WANT TO EXPLORE THE REASONS YOU CREATED ME, FATHER. I DON'T WANT TO BE WORRIED ABOUT WHAT I SHOULD DO NEXT. HELP ME FOLLOW YOU SO CLOSELY THAT I UNDERSTAND WHAT TO DO NEXT.

FILLING THE LIFE CUP

*"If they hear and serve Him, the rest of their days will be
filled with what they need and their years with peace."*
JOB 36:11

There are plenty of people who know a few things about God, and maybe they like some of the Christian music they hear on the radio, but they haven't really heard from God by reading His Word. They haven't served Him by helping others. They just like the idea of God, and they don't mind following at a distance. They aren't satisfied because they aren't close enough to hear Him. They're far enough away that they don't even know what questions to ask.

You should listen and do what God says. Picture the rest of your life as a cup that God can keep filling, giving you just what you need and reminding you that you'll always have enough of God. That's a picture that can leave you satisfied.

- -

I WANT TO BE CURIOUS ENOUGH ABOUT YOU THAT I
COME CLOSE, GOD. HELP ME FOLLOW CLOSE ENOUGH
TO HEAR AND THINK LONG ENOUGH ABOUT WHAT YOU
SAY TO UNDERSTAND WHAT I SHOULD DO NEXT.

THE TENT FIXER

I am not saying I need anything. I have learned to be happy with whatever I have. I know how to get along with little and how to live when I have much.
PHILIPPIANS 4:11–12

Paul was an apostle. He had a second job too. He made and fixed tents. Lots of people came to have Paul work on their tents. Sometimes there was plenty to do so Paul had more than enough. Other times there weren't many people who needed their tents fixed. Paul was learning lessons with every stitch and every new job. Sometimes he would have plenty and sometimes he wouldn't, but that didn't change God's love for him.

Paul could be satisfied because he knew the purpose for his life was more than how many customers he had or how much money he earned. God loved Paul, and Paul knew that was worth more than the next big job.

- -

A JOB IS ONLY SOMETHING TO DO UNLESS I DO MY WORK FOR YOU, FATHER. WHEN I DO THAT, HELP ME TO BE SATISFIED, KNOWING THAT YOU GAVE ME A JOB AND YOUR LOVE IS YOUR BEST PROMISE.

NO MORE DISCONTENT

A God-like life gives us much when we are happy for what we have. We came into this world with nothing. For sure, when we die, we will take nothing with us. If we have food and clothing, let us be happy.

1 TIMOTHY 6:6–8

If being content is being satisfied with what you have, then discontentment is the feeling that you always need more and can't understand why you don't have it. But discontentment never stops long enough to enjoy what God has already given. It always feels cheated. Nothing is ever good enough. And that kind of thinking distracts you from joy, peace, and God's better plan.

When you're content, you find there are actually more gifts you've been ignoring, more life than you've been living, and more smiles that start showing up on your face.

Be brave enough to be content. Go beyond wanting more stuff to wanting more of God.

- -

I DON'T WANT TO BE SOMEONE WHO THINKS THAT YOUR GIFTS AREN'T GOOD ENOUGH, GOD. HELP ME THANK YOU FOR EVERYTHING EVEN WHEN I DON'T KNOW WHAT TO DO WITH YOUR GOOD GIFTS YET. YOU CAN HELP ME LEARN.

BECOMING NEW

Your new life should be full of loving-pity.
You should be kind to others and have no pride.
Be gentle and be willing to wait for others.
COLOSSIANS 3:12

You probably don't like it when other people act like they're more important that you are. This is called pride, and God isn't a fan. If you don't like it when you see pride in the way someone acts, imagine how much it bothers God when people He wants to help act like they don't need Him. It's even worse when they act like they're better than most people and expect God to accept them automatically.

The new life God gave you means that you should become new. That's hard to do when you try to make people feel less important than you think you are. God says, "Be kind to others and have no pride." Then He says, "Be gentle and be willing to wait for others." Doesn't that sound like it's important to God to think about others before yourself?

- -

BEING BRAVE SOMETIMES MEANS TRYING SOMETHING DIFFERENT, FATHER. YOU WANT ME TO THINK OF OTHERS AS IMPORTANT TO YOU, SO THEY SHOULD BE IMPORTANT TO ME TOO.

STOP THINKING ABOUT YOURSELF

When pride comes, then comes shame, but
wisdom is with those who have no pride.
PROVERBS 11:2

The pride you might feel in yourself is harmful for good reasons. It's possible that someone is better at something you're proud of, and you could be missing out on friendships because you won't see value in the other person. Being prideful tells God that you don't think He's as important as He used to be. When you begin to think these things, God says a full supply of shame is heading your way.

The wise response is humility—thinking of others as more important than yourself (see Philippians 2:3). When you don't try to convince people you're better, there's less competition and more cooperation. You might even stop thinking about yourself so you can spend more time helping others and loving God.

- -

DEMANDING THE MOST IMPORTANT PLACE IS NOT WHAT YOU WANT ME TO DO, GOD. YOU DON'T WANT ME TO MAKE OTHERS FEEL BAD OR TREAT YOU AS IF YOU'RE LESS IMPORTANT. HELP ME CHOOSE HUMILITY BECAUSE REAL LIFE IS ALL ABOUT YOU.

NO PRIDE, PLEASE

Let yourself be brought low before the Lord.
Then He will lift you up and help you.
JAMES 4:10

You cannot compete with God. Sure, you're pretty creative, but you haven't created the world. You have written something people like, but you didn't invent language. God did both. He rescues, forgives, and adopts anyone who wants to be part of His family. You're important, but God will always be more important.

Being prideful doesn't make sense. You might be good at playing basketball, but you wouldn't want to challenge a professional basketball player to a game. You'd probably be embarrassed.

Maybe that's why God doesn't like pride in His family. Pride says, "Look at me—I'm the best." But pride isn't kind, doesn't show love, and often wears the face of a bully.

Be ready and willing to serve. At the right time, God will say, *"Well done."*

- -

LEARNING TO BE HUMBLE IS HARD, FATHER. WHEN I DO SOMETHING WELL, I WANT PEOPLE TO NOTICE. I WANT THEM TO RECOGNIZE THAT MY HARD WORK WAS WORTH SOMETHING. I NEVER NEED TO WONDER IF SOMEONE NOTICES, BECAUSE YOU ALWAYS HAVE.

THE HUMBLE ONE

"The Son of Man did not come to be cared for. He came to care for others."

MARK 10:45

You've read that God will always be the most important, and it's true. But when Jesus came to earth, He didn't come saying, "Hey, serve me." Jesus served others. He washed feet, healed wounds, and fed the hungry. And Jesus died because both proud and humble people still broke God's law.

Jesus' life can help you see how beautiful *humble* can be. He didn't make people feel bad when they didn't understand what He was saying. He asked God to forgive the people even when they chose to kill Him. Jesus was humble. He knew everyone would need help, and if He spent all His time demanding to be served, then very few people would have been helped.

The life of God's Son is the best example of what it looks like to serve without gold stars, a parade, or even one "like" on social media.

- -

HELP ME REALIZE THAT THE OPINION I'M MOST INTERESTED IN IS YOURS, GOD. WHAT YOU THINK MATTERS MOST. WHAT JESUS DID ON EARTH SHOWS THAT HUMILITY IS A PERFECT CHOICE.

SOUNDING WORSE

"Whoever makes himself look more important than he is will find out how little he is worth. Whoever does not try to honor himself will be made important."

LUKE 14:11

The bad part about bragging is you can make a good story about yourself sound like the life of a superhero. You might add some fairy tale to the truth and come away with a story that is bigger and sounds better than what really happened. Not only is that lying, but someone who was with you will tell the truth, and all the good that you did will be forgotten because you lied about it. By trying to make yourself sound better, you can wind up sounding worse. Then it's hard for people to believe you when you tell them about something else you did that was really good.

The Bible puts out a warning about trying to look more important. The Bible also says that if anyone wants to praise you, it should be someone besides yourself (see Proverbs 27:2).

- -

I WANT TO DO THE RIGHT THING JUST BECAUSE IT'S THE RIGHT THING TO DO, FATHER. KEEP MY MOUTH FROM PRAISING MYSELF.

AVOID THE PRIDE WALK

What does the Lord ask of you but to do what is fair and to love kindness, and to walk without pride with your God?
MICAH 6:8

If you want a really good example to follow, read today's verse again. It can send you down a straighter path with a better choice and a new way of thinking.

This is another list of three things God wants you to do.

Do what is fair. Don't cheat, don't steal, and don't deceive.

Love kindness. You shouldn't be a bully. You shouldn't be mean. You shouldn't be rude.

Walk without pride before God. Let Him see what you choose to do. Give Him the chance to change your mind. Do your best to learn what He wants you to do.

The subject of humility can be a great choice to help you become more than brave.

- -

BRAVERY CAN HELP ME TO BE STRONG ENOUGH TO LIVE WITHOUT APPLAUSE, KNOWING THERE WILL COME A DAY WHEN YOU WILL RECOGNIZE IT, GOD. YOU ARE WHO I'M SUPPOSED TO BE DOING MY WORK FOR IN THE FIRST PLACE. HELP ME DO A GOOD JOB FOR YOU.

PEACE

[Jesus said,] "I have told you these things so you m[ay]
have peace in Me. In the world you will have muc[h]
trouble. But take hope! I have power over the worl[d.]"
JOHN 16:33

Brave boys have peace. You can be certain that God is [taking]
care of you, and therefore you don't have to worry. Wher[e worry]
goes away, there is room for peace.

The reason a brave boy like you can have peace is be[cause]
you stand up to worry and send it away. You see, worry [has]
you thinking about something that might not even happe[n, that you]
can't trust and then wonder if God is really big enough [to take]
care of the things you worry about. Peace might just mea[n that]
you trust God and know that you can relax while God h[andles it]
a way only He can.

- -

WORRYING IS EASY, FATHER. I'VE DONE IT BEFORE, AND I'LL W[ILL IT]
AGAIN. FINDING PEACE IS A LITTLE HARDER, BUT THAT'S SOME[THING]
ONLY YOU CAN GIVE ME, AND IT MEANS I WILL NEED TO BELIEV[E IN]
THE PROMISES YOU'VE ALREADY MADE. HELP ME DO THAT.

THE PEACE PROMISE

*[Jesus said,] "Peace I leave with you. My peace I give
to you. I do not give peace to you as the world gives.
Do not let your hearts be troubled or afraid."*
JOHN 14:27

Peace is a powerful gift, and God has given it to you. You may
have accepted the gift, but do you know how to use it?

You might think that peace just means nobody is arguing, but
God's peace is a promise even when you live through struggles.
You've read about joy and the fact that it doesn't mean happiness. It's a trust that God's outcome is better than what you're
going through. That's a lot like peace. You can relax because
God can be trusted. You can be calm because God is in control
and there's nothing to worry about.

If worry can't make you live longer, get taller, or feel better,
then maybe it's time to choose peace when worry seems to be
an easier decision.

THANKS FOR GIVING ME PEACE, GOD. TAKE MY WORRY. DON'T
GIVE IT BACK EVEN IF I ASK FOR IT. HELP ME TRUST YOU
TO HANDLE EVERYTHING THAT CAUSES ME TO WORRY.

THE MIDDLE OF PEACE

"You will keep the man in perfect peace whose mind is kept on You, because he trusts in You."

ISAIAH 26:3

Peace knows God can control everything. Peace believes God can be completely trusted. Peace decides to think about the God who never worries. Peace keeps busy thinking great things while it stays calm. That sounds pretty wonderful, doesn't it?

What you think about is important because it can help you find peace. When you don't trust God, then the worry you feel takes all the mental strength you have and causes you to become weak. You'll believe things that aren't true, and you won't be able to trust God because you're not sure that everything is okay. That leaves you less than calm.

When you keep thinking about how God takes care of you, He leads you to the middle of peace and can keep you there as long as you keep thinking about His good gifts.

- -

I WANT YOUR PEACE, FATHER. WITHOUT IT I CAN'T BE CALM, WON'T TRUST YOU, AND COULDN'T SURVIVE THE WORRY I FEEL. MAY MY MIND THINK ABOUT YOU SO YOU CAN BRING PEACE CLOSE.

THE PEACE BRINGER

The peace of God is much greater than the human mind can understand. This peace will keep your hearts and minds through Christ Jesus.
PHILIPPIANS 4:7

Peace. *God's peace?* You need it, probably want it, and can't understand it. Peace can be yours when it feels like everything else is falling apart. That's why it doesn't make sense to most people. When you're stressed out, it's hard to think that you don't have to be. You might even believe you should worry, but when you worry, you can't think about the God who brings peace.

Take God's gift of peace, and leave worry behind. That's how your heart and mind can turn away from worry. Stop thinking about it. Jesus can do that for you. He wants to do that for you. Will you let Him?

Brave boys seek peace because they know worry doesn't accomplish anything good.

- -

WORRY IS AN EASY CHOICE, GOD. IF IT WASN'T, THEN WHY WOULD I CHOOSE IT? WORRY DOESN'T HELP ME GET THINGS DONE. I CAN'T SEEM TO TRUST YOU. I'M OFTEN FEARFUL. HELP ME TO BE BRAVE ENOUGH TO SEEK PEACE AND STAY AWAY FROM WORRY.

WORRIES HANDLED

I will lie down and sleep in peace.
O Lord, You alone keep me safe.

PSALM 4:8

Being able to sleep through the night is a good thing. You feel rested. Your day goes better. You're happier when you sleep well. But there's something that keeps you from getting the sleep you need. Worry will do that to a boy like you.

When you worry, you spend time thinking about how bad something could be. Then you don't have enough time to sleep. When you don't get enough sleep, you begin to worry that something is wrong, and that means you sleep even less. When you don't sleep well, you also get grumpy. Then you start making bad choices.

Sometimes the best sleep you get is when you trust God. He can keep you safe. He can handle your worries. He can pay attention to the things that keep you awake at night. Brave boys welcome peace.

- -

I DON'T WANT TO WORRY, FATHER. WITH YOUR HELP, I DON'T NEED TO. I NEED PEACE, GOD. WITH YOUR HELP, I CAN GET WHAT I NEED. PLEASE HELP ME.

WHAT YOU'VE ALWAYS NEEDED

Give all your worries to Him because He cares for you.
1 PETER 5:7

You make the choice to give something away. But if someone takes that thing from you, it's not a gift, is it? Consider a toy, for example. You could give it to someone (with a parent's permission), and it would be a gift. But if someone took it from you, that would be stealing.

God will never steal your worry. If you want Him to take care of your worry, then you have to give it to Him. He gives you a very powerful reason to make the choice to give worry away. He cares for you. He loves you. He wants your worry.

Who besides God has ever made your worry something they wanted? No one. Most people have worry they need to give away. They don't need more.

God can take your worry, and then, because He knows He never needs to worry, He gets rid of it. Worry is not a treasure. Peace is priceless.

- -

I WOULD LIKE TO GIVE YOU A GIFT I DON'T NEED, GOD. TAKE MY WORRY. GIVE ME THE BETTER GIFT OF PEACE. IT'S JUST WHAT I'VE ALWAYS NEEDED.

GOOD SHARING

How great is Your loving-kindness! You have stored it up for those who fear You. You show it to those who trust in You in front of the sons of men.
PSALM 31:19

How do you decide how good God is? Who do you compare Him to? There's no comparison for God. No one will ever love as much. No one will ever be as good. Call God *great* because He is.

God loves you and has even more love stored up for you. He shows His loving-kindness to those who bravely trust His message enough to share it.

God doesn't show His love and power to cowards. Instead, He comes to the rescue of those who are brave enough to acknowledge that they know Him. Think of Shadrach, Meshach, and Abednego in the book of Daniel, chapter 3. When they refused to bow to Nebuchadnezzar's statue and chose to worship God alone, God rescued them from the fiery furnace. Can you think of other people who were brave and were rescued by God's loving-kindness?

YOU SHOW KINDNESS TO A BOY WHO HAS SINNED, FATHER. I AM THAT BOY. HELP ME LEARN FROM YOU SO I CAN SHOW KINDNESS TO OTHERS. MAY IT MAKE A DIFFERENCE IN ME AND IN THE ONE WHO SEES YOUR LOVING-KINDNESS.

GOOD TO ALL

The Lord is good to all. And His loving-
kindness is over all His works.
PSALM 145:9

The very first thing you need to know about God is that He is good. He's not just good to some; He's good to all. He doesn't just love some; He loves all. He's not just kind to a few; He's kind to all.

This is a very important thing to remember. When rain falls, God doesn't just make it fall on ground used by those who follow Him; He shares it with those who refuse to follow. When you breathe air, it's not just available to you and those you go to church with. God made air for everyone.

Every day God proves just how brave He is when He's good to those who hate Him. His love is available to all, but not everyone recognizes it yet. God doesn't give up on people. Neither should you.

- -

SOMETIMES I THINK YOU ARE ONLY GOOD BECAUSE I FOLLOW YOU, GOD. HELP ME TO REMEMBER THAT YOUR GOODNESS IS WHAT MAKES PEOPLE WANT TO FOLLOW YOU. THANKS FOR BEING SO GOOD TO ALL OF US.

GOD DOESN'T HAVE BAD DAYS

You are good and You do good. Teach me Your Law.
PSALM 119:68

Your worst mistake cannot cause God to have a bad day. He can forgive you. He can cause good to come out of your bad choices. He can (and does) work on you to make a new life after old choices. God also never decides that He's been good for too long. He won't make a bad choice.

A good reason to read the Bible and do what it says is that God's laws are always designed for good. They are good for you and good for others. Following His laws proves that you want God's goodness for others and for yourself. It shows that you trust that God knows what He is doing even when you are not so sure about what you are doing.

God is good. He does good. He wants you to do good too.

- -

THE GOOD THINGS YOU DO, FATHER, HELP ME TO SEE THAT YOU DON'T CHANGE. YOU'RE AS GOOD TODAY AS YOU WERE YESTERDAY, AND YOUR GOODNESS WILL BE WAITING WHEN I WAKE UP TOMORROW MORNING.

THE TROUBLE WITH HIDDEN BADNESS

Be sure your love is true love. Hate what is sinful. Hold on to whatever is good.
ROMANS 12:9

Love cares about other people. It isn't just being nice when it makes sense to be nice and then making fun of the person you were just nice to when they leave the room. Love loves, and that's a powerful truth.

God wants you to hate what is sinful—the things God's Word and your conscience tell you are wrong to do. What if you learned to hate sin instead of sinning and then asking for forgiveness? You can't make good choices without help, but how often do you ask for help?

If God says something is good, you should hold on to what He says is good and let go of what's bad. Stop keeping badness hidden just in case you want to use it later.

- -

YOU OFFER GOODNESS, AND SOMETIMES I OVERLOOK IT, GOD. HELP ME STAY CLOSE TO GOOD AND GIVE UP THE BAD THINGS THAT I USED TO THINK WERE NORMAL. WALK WITH ME AND TEACH ME GOOD THINGS.

STOP THE CONFUSION

We should do good to everyone. For sure, we should do good to those who belong to Christ.
GALATIANS 6:10

People don't expect Christians to do bad things, but Christians often do bad things. You should love people, but sometimes you don't. You should help, but sometimes you treat people as if they should help themselves. You should care about people, but sometimes you think only about yourself.

Do you see why the way Christians sometimes act confuses those who still need to follow God? When you act with goodness, you will model goodness to all people—those who don't love God and those who do. God can use you to help in the way He wants to help others. God might use you to be the answer to someone else's prayer.

- -

HELP ME NOT TO MAKE BAD CHOICES, FATHER. MAY THE THINGS I DECIDE TO DO BE HELPFUL. MAY THOSE DECISIONS LOOK A LOT LIKE THE DECISIONS YOU WOULD MAKE. HELP ME AGREE TO BE HELPFUL WHEN YOU WANT TO USE ME TO ANSWER A PRAYER.

GOOD LIFE STORIES

Do not let sin have power over you. Let good have power over sin!
ROMANS 12:21

Sin whispers, *Stop being good. You're missing out on so much fun.* Sin will always try to convince you that you're missing out on something, and it can be easy to believe sin. After all, when you do good it helps others, but what's in it for you? When your mind moves to this kind of thinking, sin has become more powerful in your life and it's harder for you to hear God's truth.

Let's look at what happens when you're brave enough to let God's goodness guide your choices. When you know that God's goodness helps you to be a blessing to others, then that truth suddenly becomes more powerful than the choice to sin. God's goodness can lead brave boys beyond where they are to a place where God-sized stories come to life.

- -

I DON'T WANT SIN TO TELL ME WHAT TO DO, GOD. PLEASE SEND YOUR GOODNESS WITH YOUR MESSAGE, AND HELP ME LISTEN TO YOUR DIRECTIONS FOR A GOOD LIFE.

WISDOM LEADS

The wisdom that comes from heaven is first of all pure. Then it gives peace. It is gentle and willing to obey. It is full of loving-kindness and of doing good. It has no doubts and does not pretend to be something it is not.

JAMES 3:17

You might think someone is wise just because they tell you about things you hadn't thought of before, but what if what they tell you isn't the truth? God's wisdom is different. The Bible describes it as pure. That means it's correct and without any flaws. Because His wisdom leads you to the best places, you can discover peace. When you have wisdom, you'll be kind and gentle with others and you'll be willing to follow God's laws.

When you're wise, you show goodness to others, never need to doubt God's plan, and don't have to try to convince anyone that you're something different than you are. Your life will show all these things because wisdom follows God.

- -

I WANT TO BE MORE THAN BRAVE, SO PLEASE GIVE ME WISDOM, FATHER. WHEN I ACCEPT YOUR WISDOM, I LEARN ALL THE THINGS THAT MAKE LIFE BETTER.

BECOMING WISE

The Lord gives wisdom. Much learning and understanding come from His mouth.
PROVERBS 2:6

You can learn a lot of things from many people. For example, you can learn how to play an instrument, excel at sports, or take care of pets. But all this learning isn't what wisdom is.

Does that sound confusing? Here's how it works: wisdom does something with what you learn. That means you can read this book and learn something about God and what it looks like to be a boy who is more than brave, but if you want to move from being smart to being wise, you need to do something more than just read this book.

This is a book of next steps. You have been asked to be brave. To become wise, you need to take everything you've learned about being brave and ask God to help you put the knowledge you've gained into practice. That is wisdom.

- -

YOU WANT ME TO BE WISE, AND I WANT TO BE WISE TOO, GOD.
HELP ME THINK ABOUT WAYS TO LEARN, THEN UNDERSTAND,
AND THEN DO WHAT YOU NEED ME TO DO TO BECOME WISE.

WISDOM'S CHOICE

A wise man fears God and turns away from what is sinful, but a fool is full of pride and is not careful.
PROVERBS 14:16

If you've paid attention to what you've learned the past couple of days, then it probably won't surprise you to know that one of the best things you can do to become wise is to turn your back on making choices that break God's law.

Today's verse shows you that it's possible to learn what God wants and then make a choice that says you haven't really learned anything at all. You can know that God wants you to be humble yet still act with pride. You can know there are things you shouldn't do yet do them anyway.

Learning can teach you the right thing to do, but it's wisdom that helps you to actually do the right thing. Learning can teach you that God should be respected, but it's wisdom that shows God respect.

- -

I WANT TO RESPECT YOU BECAUSE I'VE LEARNED THAT YOU ARE WORTH RESPECTING, FATHER. I WANT TO BE CAREFUL IN WHAT I DO BECAUSE I'VE LEARNED THAT YOUR LAWS ARE WORTH OBEYING.

NEVER WRONG TO ASK

*If you do not have wisdom, ask God for it. He is always ready
to give it to you and will never say you are wrong for asking.*
JAMES 1:5

Wisdom isn't just for boys who spend lots of time thinking about what they learn. It's for boys who are brave enough to ask God for help. He doesn't want you to be confused. He doesn't want you to learn and not know what to do with what you know. God isn't interested in making you think He won't help. *Ask.* God can help you become wise.

This same God doesn't want you to decide to ask only when you've tried everything you can to become wise on your own. Ask early and keep asking. The Bible even says you'll never be wrong to ask God for wisdom. So get ready to ask.

- -

I'M LEARNING, BUT I'M NOT WISE YET, GOD. TEACH ME SO
I CAN LEARN. THEN KEEP TEACHING SO I'LL KNOW WHAT
TO DO AFTER I LEARN. BECAUSE IT'S NEVER WRONG
TO ASK, WILL YOU HELP ME TO BECOME WISE?

HE'S ALWAYS WISE

God's riches are so great! The things He knows and His wisdom are so deep! No one can understand His thoughts. No one can understand His ways.

ROMANS 11:33

God is always at work in people's lives. Some are learning from Him. Some are running away from Him. Some are becoming wise.

Don't expect God to do things the way you might. His way of doing things may be very different. God always acts on what He knows. That means He's always wise.

On your own, you can't understand everything God wants to teach. He uses His Spirit to help you understand what you learn so you can become wise.

The reason you need God's help to become wise is that no one can teach you what only God knows. It's true, you can learn many things, and this book is one way to learn, but God's wisdom is a gift that He wants to give that's just for you. Remember, God's wisdom is deep, His thoughts may be hard to understand, and His ways may be different than yours.

- -

I WANT TO BE MORE LIKE YOU, FATHER,
SO HELP ME TO SPEND MORE TIME WITH YOU.

113

THE WISEST TRADE

*Trust in the Lord with all your heart, and do
not trust in your own understanding.*
PROVERBS 3:5

The things you understand may only answer simple questions. For instance, you might know that you can get water from the faucet, but where does that water come from, how is it stored, and where does it go once it goes down the drain?

You can know God is good, kind, and loving, but do you know how good He is, do you know why He's kind, and do you know the real power of His love?

Believe simply, but be assured that there's always more to know. Your understanding may not take in the full story. You can be certain that God can be trusted. Give Him all that you are so that you can have all that He gives. It will be the wisest trade you ever make.

- -

LET ME TRUST YOU, GOD. I DON'T WANT TO TRUST WHAT I KNOW, BECAUSE THAT COULD MAKE ME BELIEVE SOMETHING THAT'S NOT TRUE. SPEAK TO ME THROUGH THE BIBLE AND LET ME HEAR WHAT YOU NEED ME TO KNOW.

A SERIOUS DECISION

*How can a young man keep his way
pure? By living by Your Word.*
PSALM 119:9

Purity is another way for you to be more than brave. It starts with bravery, because deciding to set yourself apart to God isn't a decision that every boy will make. Those who don't make this decision will try to make you think it's a silly thing to do, but it's a serious decision and it's a choice God wants you to make.

If you want to be pure and holy, set apart for God to use, then make your choices by knowing what the Bible says. This is something you've read a lot in this book, but if you want to be more than brave, then the Bible is the guidebook you need for a life that God can use to make a difference.

It's pretty wonderful that the Bible pays attention to "a young man." Perhaps God knew you would read this and that it would make a difference for you.

- -

I WANT TO CHOOSE TO BE USEFUL TO YOU. HELP ME TO BE PURE, FATHER. HELP ME PAY ATTENTION TO THE WORDS I READ IN THE BIBLE.

WILLING TO BE PURE

Let no one show little respect for you because you are young. Show other Christians how to live by your life. They should be able to follow you in the way you talk and in what you do. Show them how to live in faith and in love and in holy living.
1 TIMOTHY 4:12

Don't let anyone tell you that you're too young to make the choice to follow God. The Bible tells you that a boy like yourself can show other people how to be pure and set apart for God's use.

You may not have known it, but a brave boy can be an example to those who want to walk, talk, and act like a Christian. You can show them what it looks like to trust God, how to love people, and how to be willing to be pure.

- -

YOU ARE GOD, AND YOU MADE BOYS TO BE BRAVE ENOUGH TO BE PURE. I WANT TO HELP PEOPLE SEE WHAT IT LOOKS LIKE TO BE WILLING TO DO WHAT YOU WANT, WHICH IS THE BEST THING ANYONE COULD EVER DO. HELP ME LOOK LIKE THAT.

CLEAN HEART

*Make a clean heart in me, O God. Give me
a new spirit that will not be moved.*
PSALM 51:10

Your heart is where God lives. It's where God's Spirit teaches. It can be filled with good things. But that same heart can tell you lies, hold on to hurt, and store sin. It's hard for God to help you when you don't have enough room in your heart for Him to work. He wants your whole heart, not just a spare room.

Use today's verse as a prayer: "Make a clean heart in me, O God. Give me a new spirit that will not be moved."

Ask for forgiveness, and invite sin to move out. Believe what God says is true, and discover that the lies that find a home in your heart don't feel welcome. Love others, and discover less hurt in your heart. Ask for God's help in making the best choices.

- -

I ONLY HAVE ROOM IN MY HEART FOR YOU, FATHER. HELP ME STOP ASKING POOR GUESTS TO LIVE THERE. SIN DOESN'T LIKE YOU, AND YOU DON'T LIKE SIN. MAKE YOUR HOME IN MY HEART.

TODAY'S BEST CHOICE

Come close to God and He will come close to you. Wash your hands, you sinners. Clean up your hearts, you who want to follow the sinful ways of the world and God at the same time.
JAMES 4:8

Someone wants you to be close to God. That's why you have this book. It was probably a gift, and you may be reading it with a family member, maybe with another brother.

God is closer than the pages of this book. If you come close to Him, then He will come close to you. He doesn't want you to be the same after reading this page as you were when you started.

You see, every day you have a choice to make. You can either follow God or follow ways that lead to sin. You can't do both at the same time. *You just can't.*

Let God clean your heart, come close, and lead you to today's best choice.

- -

YOU ARE WELCOME, GOD. MAKE MY HEART YOUR HOME, AND MAKE MY HEART CLEAN. IT MAY BE UNFAIR TO ASK A GUEST TO CLEAN UP BEFORE THEY MOVE IN, BUT IT'S WHAT EVERYONE NEEDS MOST.

TRUTH FROM A DISTANCE

The mind that thinks only of ways to please the sinful old self is fighting against God. It is not able to obey God's Laws. It never can.
ROMANS 8:7

There's something to remember when you want to be set apart so God can use you. The old guests that used to live in your heart will show up from time to time to remind you of the days when you did what they wanted. They can make your old life sound fun and tempt you to live that way again. Don't put out the welcome mat.

If you only think of doing what pleases your old self, you will find yourself fighting against God. The old life that you left was never able to follow God. It never will be able to. All it can do is leave you with bad decisions and make you think of God as someone who has never been interested in you. Nothing could be further from the truth.

- -

PURITY MAKES FOLLOWING YOU A FULL-TIME JOB, FATHER. WHEN I'M NOT SERIOUS ABOUT FOLLOWING YOU, IT BECOMES MUCH EASIER TO BREAK YOUR LAWS, BECOME SELFISH, AND TURN AWAY WHEN YOU WANT ME TO FOLLOW. I NEED YOUR HELP.

THE LIFE HE'S ALWAYS LIVED

"Be holy, for I am holy."
1 PETER 1:16

Today there's one more part of purity you should know. God doesn't ask you to be set apart without being set apart Himself. He chose to be something different for people who might choose not to trust, follow, or obey.

God is holy, and He wants you to be holy—set apart for Him to use. The life He wants for you is the life He's always lived. He knew what it would take to be holy, and He has given you everything you need to be holy. Like everything He asks, He provides the example for you to follow.

Be a brave boy following a brave God who offers an adventure that provides a reason to do good things, love others, and know He has something very special that only you can do. Be holy. That's what God does.

- -

WHY WOULD I BE INTERESTED IN DOING ANYTHING LESS THAN FOLLOWING YOU, GOD? BUT THERE ARE TIMES WHEN I WANT WHAT YOU'VE SAID IS OFF LIMITS. HELP ME CHOOSE TO BE SET APART SO THAT WHEN YOU SEND ME ON MY NEXT ADVENTURE, I'M READY AND WILLING.

STOP GIVING UP THE GOOD

Do not let yourselves get tired of doing good. If we do not give up, we will get what is coming to us at the right time.
GALATIANS 6:9

Giving up is easy. If you play baseball and it's not easy, you give up. If you want to learn to play the guitar but your fingers can't seem to find the right string, you give up. When a friendship doesn't seem to be working, you give up.

There are things that you should give up. That might include bitterness, anger, and selfishness. God's Word gives a good example of things you shouldn't give up on—love, joy, peace, being kind, being good, having faith, being gentle, and being the boss over our own desires.

When you refuse to give up on the good, you can claim God's promises that a better day is coming, you'll get better with practice, and you get to spend forever with God.

- -

I NEED PATIENCE, FATHER. WHEN I DON'T HAVE IT,
I GIVE UP ON SOME OF THE THINGS YOU'VE ASKED
ME TO DO. TEACH ME TO WAIT FOR YOU.

PATIENT PRAYERS

Do not worry. Learn to pray about everything. Give thanks to God as you ask Him for what you need.
PHILIPPIANS 4:6

You might really want something. It's the kind of thing you've thought about, read about, and imagined yourself owning. What if you prayed about it? God might ask you to be patient. He might say no, but He could also say yes.

Patience and a wish don't work well together no matter what movies and storybooks tell you. Patience and prayer is a much better choice. While you're being patient, you can thank God before He ever answers your prayer. That type of prayer shows that you believe God can be trusted and that you're willing to wait for His answer.

Trust makes worry go away, prayer teaches patience, and thankfulness reminds you that God is good. Remember that sometimes even delays are God's answer to your prayers.

- -

DELAYS ARE HARD, GOD. A DRIVE-THROUGH MEANS GETTING FOOD FAST, ORDERING ONLINE MEANS QUICK DELIVERY, AND IF I'M THIRSTY I GET A DRINK. I DON'T EVEN HAVE TO WAIT. TEACH ME TO ASK FOR YOUR HELP AND BE PATIENT UNTIL IT SHOWS UP.

GOD HAS PLENTY OF PATIENCE

Love does not give up.
1 CORINTHIANS 13:4

Two days ago you read about not giving up. You know that good things come to those who are patient. Today you'll see that the main reason you don't give up comes down to one thing: love. That includes God's love for you, your love for God, God's love for others, and your love for others. Maybe love doesn't give up because it cares more, serves more, and waits longer. Love is patient.

Imagine if God didn't love everyone. It would be easy for Him to give up on people and not give mercy because His love was limited. God would have to either love some or love all. Thankfully, the thing that made sense to Him was to love all, be patient with all, and offer forgiveness to all. And He also gives plenty of time to accept His offer.

Let's end the way we began: love does not give up.

- -

YOU'RE SO PATIENT WITH ME, FATHER. THAT MUST MEAN THAT YOU LOVE ME. HELP ME LOVE PEOPLE THAT WAY.

STRENGTH FROM PATIENCE

They who wait upon the Lord will get new strength. They will rise up with wings like eagles. They will run and not get tired. They will walk and not become weak.

ISAIAH 40:31

Today's verse is pretty wonderful. You've probably heard it before. This verse tells you about the great things that wait for you when you wait patiently for God's answer.

You get new strength. When you serve the Lord, He gives you the strength to do the job He calls you to do.

Rise up. God will give you power to move up to a better place than where you are. But you may have to be patient while rising up to reach that place.

Run and not get tired. Patience can help you endure.

Walk and not become weak. Keep walking; there's no reason to give up.

Waiting can make you strong. Patience can help you trust. Endurance can make you wise.

- -

LIFE IS HARD, BUT THERE'S SOMETHING WAITING FOR ME. HELP ME TO BE PATIENT, GOD. GIVE ME THE STRENGTH I NEED, THE RECOLLECTION OF YOUR GOOD PROMISES, AND WISDOM TO ENDURE THE STRUGGLES I MAY FACE BEFORE YOUR BETTER DAY FOR ME ARRIVES.

WILLING TO WAIT

Rest in the Lord and be willing to wait for Him.
PSALM 37:7

When you're told to be patient, you might use all your free time worrying about what you want and when you might get it. You already know that God doesn't want you to worry, right? So when you need to be patient, you must also be willing to rest in the Lord, trusting Him to take care of things in His perfect timing.

Patience makes it possible to do what you need to do today without worrying about tomorrow. It helps you focus on what's happening right now while looking forward to God's good plan.

It's braver to be patient than it is to be fearful. You can be brave. Don't give up.

- -

THERE'S MORE TO PATIENCE THAN I THOUGHT, FATHER. IT WOULD BE EASY TO SAY I'M BEING PATIENT WHILE I'M WORRIED ABOUT WHETHER I'M WASTING MY TIME. THAT'S NOT TRUST, AND IT'S NOT BEING PATIENT. HELP ME DISCOVER REST WHILE I WAIT FOR YOU.

HEADLINES

The Lord is not slow about keeping His promise as some people think. He is waiting for you. . . . He wants all people to be sorry for their sins and turn from them.
2 Peter 3:9

God is where you go to get good news. You can read headlines like "God made humans and called it good" or "God's love paves the way for forgiveness."

Then you read the headline "God agrees to be patient," and you realize that God has not asked you to do something He won't do. He wants you to be patient with others, and then He shows that He is patient with others. Some people still need to follow Him. So God is patient while He waits for them to recognize that they need Him. He endures because He loves people enough to give them time to discover His good news headlines.

THANK YOU FOR BEING PATIENT WITH EVERYONE, GOD. I DON'T ALWAYS FOLLOW. I DON'T ALWAYS TRUST. BUT YOU WAIT PATIENTLY AS I DISCOVER WHERE TO LOOK FOR GOOD NEWS THAT BRINGS ME TO YOU. THIS IS HOW I LEARN. THIS IS HOW YOU MAKE ME WISE.

THE GENTLE CYCLE

Be gentle and kind to all people.
TITUS 3:2

Sometimes when you're having a bad day, you let people know how bad you feel by treating them the way you've been treated—not the way you want to be treated. You say mean things, you don't show kindness, and you're not very much fun to be around.

God teaches something better. Don't treat people the way you feel like treating them. Instead, "Be gentle and kind to all people." That sounds just like the way most people want to be treated. It's the way you want to be treated.

God was pretty clear, wasn't He? He didn't say some people, friends, or family. God said *all* people.

This is the brave choice of gentleness, and it's a choice you can make. God is pleased when you do. It's what He wants from you, and He can help you do it.

- -

WHEN I'M CONFUSED ABOUT HOW I SHOULD TREAT OTHERS I ONLY NEED TO THINK OF YOU, FATHER. THE GENTLENESS YOU SHARE ISN'T MEANT TO BE KEPT, BUT GIVEN AWAY. HELP ME REFUSE TO KEEP WHAT YOU WANT ME TO SHARE.

AN ANSWER NO ONE EXPECTS

*A gentle answer turns away anger, but
a sharp word causes anger.*
PROVERBS 15:1

Say something unkind, and someone will follow your example. What they say might make you want to say something that's even more unkind. If you do, you'd be playing a game where everyone loses and everyone's angry.

God has a very different idea, and when you choose this idea, it's possible for everyone to win. If someone says something unkind, you can say something gentle to them. When they are angry, don't become angry. Your response is like a gas tank without fuel. When you don't add fuel, the "anger engine" stops running.

Gentleness is bravery in action. Why? Every part of you wants to get even because responding in anger is the normal response. But gentleness is a response no one expects. Maybe that's why God wants you to use a gentle answer.

- -

FATHER, THE WORLD IS ALREADY ANGRY ENOUGH, SO
PLEASE GIVE ME THE STRENGTH TO BE GENTLE
IN THE WAY I ACT AND IN THE WORDS I SPEAK.
HELP MY GENTLE WORDS TO STOP ANGER.

YOUNG AND GENTLE

Be gentle when you try to teach those
who are against what you say.
2 TIMOTHY 2:25

The Bible says that even when you're young, you can teach people the right way to live. It also says that young boys like you can look for (and find) purity.

What do you do when you tell people what you're learning about God and they tell you they don't believe anything you say about God? You love God, right? You believe what He says. You think it's important enough to share. You want others to know what you know.

It can be frustrating when people think you don't know what you're talking about. They might say they think God is a made-up story. And that can make you sad, confused, or even angry.

Even when people don't agree with what you believe, God wants you to be gentle. You don't have to make people believe in God; you just have to tell them the truth—gently.

- -

YOU DON'T NEED MY HELP TO LET PEOPLE KNOW ABOUT YOU, FATHER. BUT YOU ASK ME TO SHARE. GIVE ME GENTLE WORDS TO SHARE WHAT I KNOW. YOU DO THE REST.

129

HOW TO SHARE

[Jesus said,] "Follow My teachings and learn from Me. I am gentle and do not have pride. You will have rest for your souls."
MATTHEW 11:29

Jesus spent a long time teaching His disciples. They got to learn from God's Son. They could see how He taught and learn what He said, but just in case they missed it, Jesus told them that His life was their best lesson. Yes, Jesus wanted them to tell others what He had said, but He wanted them to learn how to say it.

If the only thing Jesus wanted people to know was what He said, then the disciples could have told people His words in a way that seemed angry because they thought people weren't paying attention to Jesus' teaching. But Jesus was gentle and humble. He wasn't rude and angry. That's how He wants you to be when you tell people about Him. And You can relax because anger won't be part of the way you act around people who need to know Jesus.

- -

MAY MY WORDS HONOR YOU AND RESPECT OTHERS, GOD. HELP ME LEARN TO SPEAK GENTLY.

A BOY'S ANGER

My Christian brothers, you know everyone should listen much and speak little. He should be slow to become angry. A man's anger does not allow him to be right with God.
JAMES 1:19–20

It's not wrong to get angry, but anger should not be your first choice. You can be angry when you see people do bad things to other people, but don't stay angry. The longer you're angry, the harder it is to make good decisions. You want people to pay for what they did, you want to get back at that person, and you can refuse to forgive them.

So use your ears to listen. Don't speak as much. You may not know the whole story, so don't get angry thinking you do. Anger isn't gentle, and when it hangs around it looks very little like God's response and can even separate you from God.

IT'S NOT HARD TO GET ANGRY, FATHER. SO HELP ME LISTEN MORE THAN I SPEAK, LOVE MORE THAN I JUDGE, AND SHOW KINDNESS MORE THAN ANGER.

GENTLENESS ON DISPLAY

Let all people see how gentle you are.
PHILIPPIANS 4:5

Gentleness is not your secret superpower. It is a characteristic that everyone can see. You should be gentle so often that when people think of you, they think of how gentle you are and wonder what makes you that way. You get to be more than brave when you tell the story of a gentle God who has made a difference in you.

Think about why gentleness is so important. Do you like to be around angry people? When they speak with meanness in their voices, does that make you want to trust them? No, but gentleness is attractive and causes others to want to be around you and to get to know the God who lives in you.

Gentleness is what lets you be happy when people are happy and sad when they are sad. It pays attention to people and what they are going through. It pays attention to the way God wants you to treat them.

- -

I WANT TO BE SO GENTLE THAT PEOPLE NOTICE YOU,
GOD. MAY THE DIFFERENCE YOU MAKE IN ME MAKE
A DIFFERENCE IN THOSE YOU LET ME MEET.

EVERYTHING GRATITUDE

*In everything give thanks. This is what God
wants you to do because of Christ Jesus.*
1 THESSALONIANS 5:18

Thanksgiving is celebrated each year because it's important to have a day when people can remember to thank God for the good things He does. But did you know you can thank Him for things you don't think are good? For instance, you can thank Him for an upcoming test, not because you want to take the test, but because the test itself means you are learning. You can thank God that someone said something mean or rude, because it means God has given you the chance to give a gentle response.

Today's verse says that God wants you to give thanks because of Jesus. That could mean that you are thankful because Jesus wants you to be thankful. You could also be thankful because Jesus did something for you that you could never do for yourself. Both reasons are part of "everything" God wants you to be thankful for.

- -

I THANK YOU BECAUSE YOU'RE KIND, FATHER. EVERYTHING YOU
DO IS WORTHY OF MY THANKS. I WANT TO REMEMBER TO THANK
YOU EVERY DAY, NOT JUST ON THANKSGIVING.

HE MAKES YOU BRAVE

Give thanks to the Lord for He is good!
His loving-kindness lasts forever!
PSALM 107:1

If God's love, kindness, and goodness last forever, that means they will never end. It also means they have always been. God was loving, kind, and good even before you were born. So you can be assured that there will never be a time in your life when God won't still be loving, kind, and good.

Brave boys are thankful because they know that God is the One who makes them brave. You see, brave boys don't become brave without help. Thanking God for making you brave is proof that you know who helped you get to where you are.

God didn't stop with bravery either. Just think of all the things He helps you with. You'll never have a good reason to stop thanking Him.

- -

YOU TEACH ME SO MANY GOOD THINGS, GOD. I'M GRATEFUL FOR EVERY LESSON THAT HELPS ME BECOME MORE THAN BRAVE, WISER THAN SMART, AND MORE HELPFUL THAN JUST HAVING GOOD INTENTIONS.

GOD TAKES CARE OF YOU

Go into His gates giving thanks and into His holy place
with praise. Give thanks to Him. Honor His name.
PSALM 100:4

When you pray, you get to meet with God. When you meet with God, you should think of something you're thankful for. Bring God a gift of praise. Show up with honor.

Everything you are and everything you'll one day be started when God breathed your name. He's taken care of you your whole life, and that includes hard times. He doesn't promise that you'll never struggle, but He does promise to be with you when you do struggle. Go ahead and thank Him. It's the right thing to do, and it lets God know that the good things He does mean something to you. Thank God. Praise Him. Give Him the gift of honor.

- -

FOR YOUR GREAT GIFTS, THANK YOU, FATHER. FOR LOVE THAT
ACCEPTS ME, THANK YOU. FOR A FUTURE WITH YOU, I'M GRATEFUL.
FOR TEACHING ME, WALKING WITH ME, AND BEING PATIENT WITH
ME, THANKS. FOR ALL THAT I'LL ONE DAY BE, I PRAISE YOU,
AND I WANT YOU TO BE HONORED BY WHAT I DO TODAY.

NEVER STOP

Keep praying. Keep watching! Be thankful always.
COLOSSIANS 4:2

Pray. Then what? *Keep praying.* Pay attention. Then what? *Keep paying attention.* Be thankful. Then what? *Never stop being thankful.*

These are not onetime events. You don't mark them off your list, thinking you've done all you can do. And you don't treat them as duties you have to do even when you don't want to pray, watch, or be thankful. There's a difference between doing something because it's your job and doing it because you just can't help yourself. God wants you to be so amazed when you talk with Him that it's easy to bring thanks with you. And you can do that, because when you pay attention you see so many things that God does.

Remember God's goodness, and let God know that He's more than wonderful to you.

- -

I'M THANKFUL FOR THE THINGS YOU DO, GOD. I'M PAYING ATTENTION TO THE THINGS YOU'RE DOING, AND I'M AMAZED. THANK YOU!

ASK GOD FOR HELP

I will praise the name of God with song. And I will give Him great honor with much thanks.
PSALM 69:30

You might think you have to try as hard as you can to do everything yourself *before* God is willing to help. You might think that it's wrong to ask God for help before you try to figure things out on your own. That idea isn't in the Bible, although some people think it is.

God helps people who ask Him for help. You don't have to wait until you make three good choices in a row, help enough around the house, or even show more kindness to your family. He can help even when you make mistakes or are unkind or unhelpful. Just remember to ask for God's forgiveness and for God's help.

Choose to praise God and thank Him for His help. He does so much for you.

- -

I NEED YOUR HELP, FATHER. I KNOW I DON'T ALWAYS ASK, BUT I NEED TO. I DON'T ALWAYS THANK YOU, BUT I SHOULD. I DON'T ALWAYS PRAISE YOU, BUT YOU'RE WORTHY. YOU'RE A GOOD GOD. HELP ME TO REMEMBER THAT AND THEN TO TELL YOU HOW GRATEFUL I AM.

GOOD. PERFECT. JESUS.

Whatever is good and perfect comes to us from God. He is the One Who made all light. He does not change. No shadow is made by His turning.

JAMES 1:17

Good things come from God. Jesus is good—and perfect. No wonder God sent Him to be your gift of rescue. He gave you the gift of light because He is light. God doesn't change His mind about you; He loves you. He doesn't cast a shadow because He is the Light of the world—no light is brighter than Him.

If God sounds pretty wonderful, then tell Him how you feel about Him. Thank Him for the good things. Praise Him for the perfect things. Worship Him for helping you see the truth of a changeless God.

Be brave enough to admit that God is great and worth your gratitude. No one can do what God does. It's okay to get excited about Him.

- -

I FEEL THANKFUL, GOD. YOU'VE THOUGHT OF EVERYTHING. THAT INCLUDES ME. HELP ME TO REMEMBER THAT YOU'RE GOOD AND PERFECT AND THAT YOU LOVE ME. THANK YOU FOR GIVING ME SO MUCH MORE THAN I DESERVE.

THE JOY GOD FEELS

"We must remember what the Lord Jesus said, 'We are more happy when we give than when we receive.' "
ACTS 20:35

Get a gift and you will probably be happy. Give a gift and somehow it's an even better feeling. Sometimes you can give a gift, knowing that it's not just what someone wants but something they need. You can give a gift, knowing that it's the kind of thing God has done for you.

Jesus said that giving would be like that. It helps you experience the joy that God feels when He gives. This kind of generosity asks selfishness to look for a different place to sit. You can't be generous and selfish at the same time. Selfishness *wants* and generosity *wants to give*. Giving is one of the best things you can do to change the way you think about other people.

- -

I COULD SPEND A LOT OF TIME THINKING ABOUT WHAT I WANT, FATHER. YOU WANT ME TO THINK ABOUT OTHER PEOPLE AND WHAT THEY NEED. GENEROSITY BRINGS JOY WITH THE SURPRISE, AND WHEN I GIVE, PEOPLE GET TO SEE THE WAY YOU DO THINGS.

GIVE TO THE LORD

He who shows kindness to a poor man gives to the
Lord and He will pay him in return for his good act.
PROVERBS 19:17

There will always be someone who has less than you do. There will always be someone you can help. There will always be an opportunity to be kind. When you take the opportunity to be kind and show generosity to someone who could use a little help, God says that what you've done is like lending to Him.

When God repays, it's not like getting a dollar for taking out the trash, raking leaves, or cleaning your room. In fact, when God repays, it might never be in extra cash. He might pay back peace, satisfaction, or joy for the kindness you offer other people.

When you are generous, God is pleased, you feel good, and the needs of others are met.

- -

I WOULD BE HONORED TO BE A PART OF THE WAY YOU ANSWER PRAYER, GOD. WHEN YOU HAVE SOMEONE WHO NEEDS HELP, I CAN GIVE. WOULD YOU INTRODUCE ME TO THEM? YOU CAN HELP ME HELP THOSE WHO NEED HELP.

THE MEANING OF RICH

"Wherever your riches are, your heart will be there also."
MATTHEW 6:21

If what makes you feel rich has anything to do with *things*, then you probably need to rethink what you believe it means to be rich. If it's a house, a toy, or even a bike, then you may be thinking that being rich means owning things that won't last. That makes it seem silly to think you're rich when you own things, doesn't it? Maybe there's a better idea.

God thinks you're rich when you take the gifts He offers. When you do, you can forgive and help heal a broken heart, trust God and recognize His love for you, and be generous and discover that God has even more to share with you.

When you believe that you're rich because of those gifts, then you'll begin to enjoy spending time with the Gift Giver. He has always wanted to spend time with you.

- -

HELP ME MAKE DECISIONS THAT ARE GENEROUS BECAUSE YOU'RE GENEROUS, FATHER. HELP ME GIVE BECAUSE YOU GAVE. HELP ME LOVE BECAUSE LOVE WAS THE GIFT THAT MEANT I COULD MEET YOU.

HE LOVES PEOPLE LIKE YOU

God loves a man who gives because he wants to give.
2 CORINTHIANS 9:7

You were born with an unwillingness to share. You didn't want anyone to touch your toys. You told other people, "Hey, that's mine!" You have been jealous when someone took something you wanted. It's not hard to keep what you can share. Most people do.

But God said that He loves people like you when you learn enough about Him to know that being generous is exactly what He does. When you want to give to others and to God, you're a brave boy moving beyond selfishness. You might just be learning that you'll never be able to give more than God has given you. *Never.*

There's joy in generosity, and it shows up before, during, and after you share.

- -

WHEN I CHOOSE TO BE GENEROUS, I WANT IT TO BE BECAUSE I WANT TO SHARE, GOD. WHEN I FEEL LIKE I HAVE TO GIVE, I'M NEVER AS HAPPY AS WHEN I REALLY WANT TO SHARE SOMETHING WITH SOMEONE. YOU WANT TO GIVE. YOU HAVE. YOUR GIFTS ARE AMAZING.

GIFTS DISCOVERED

The man who gives much will have much, and
he who helps others will be helped himself.
PROVERBS 11:25

You might think that what you earn is yours, and if you want something, you work hard to get it. That seems to be the way it works with money and things. God said something very different. If you give more, you'll have more. If you give love, you'll get love. If you are kind, you'll discover more kindness. If you help others, you'll receive help.

Generosity requires that you love others. Loving others requires bravery, and bravery begins when you trust God. The Bible doesn't teach that you will always get back the same thing you give. You can give time, you can share your skills, and you can listen to the hurts people feel. You can feel repaid immediately because you're satisfied that your help meant something, but there can be more repayment to come, and it will probably be gifts you never expected. They will be gifts God sends to you.

I WANT TO RECOGNIZE YOUR GIFTS, FATHER, BUT I WANT TO GIVE BECAUSE I LOVE YOU ENOUGH TO DO WHAT YOU ASK.

A WAY TO BE REMEMBERED

Many will give thanks to God for sending gifts through us.
2 CORINTHIANS 9:11

Ten years from now you will be older and hopefully wiser. You might be reliable and loyal. How do you want people to remember who you are right now? To improve their memories, you have some brave decisions to make, and you can start making them today.

If you want people to think of you as generous, then you need to set selfishness on the bench. If you want kindness to be the memory, then sideline revenge. If you want to be remembered as loyal, then shut the lights out on unreliable choices.

What would it be like if one brave boy was used by God to help change the hearts of other boys? Those boys might just thank God for sending gifts through you. What a way to be remembered!

- -

PEOPLE REMEMBER YOU AS BEING A GIFT-GIVING GOD. BECAUSE YOU TEACH ME, MAY I MAKE CHOICES THAT CAUSE OTHERS TO THANK YOU FOR SENDING YOUR GIFTS AND ALLOWING SOMEONE LIKE ME TO DELIVER THOSE GIFTS.

INTEGRITY

A poor man who walks in his honor is better
than a rich man who is sinful in his ways.
PROVERBS 28:6

Integrity is a word that means you make excellent choices based on a set of good moral principles—the guidelines in the Bible. You make good choices even when it's hard. You're honest. You choose right living. You follow God. You love people.

Integrity will give up what is wrong to do the right thing—even if it's harder. Having integrity means that you will be the same good person and make the same good choices all the time. You will be trustworthy and will act like a leader who is willing to help others instead of bossing them around. You will honor your parents, teachers, and other adults. You will speak the truth and stand up for what is right.

You can have very few things and choose integrity. You can have a lot of things and choose to be dishonest. You need to know that the opposite is also true.

Brave boys choose integrity.

- -

I WANT TO MAKE A DAILY CHOICE TO LIVE AS SOMEONE WHO HAS INTEGRITY, FATHER. MAY I BE BRAVE ENOUGH TO MAKE GOOD CHOICES. MAY I BE TRUSTWORTHY AS I LEARN FROM A TRUSTWORTHY GOD.

THE WAY YOU HAVE LIVED

*If men speak against you, they will be ashamed when
they see the good way you have lived as a Christian.*
1 PETER 3:16

Has someone ever accused you of doing something you didn't do? It felt pretty horrible, didn't it? It seemed like they didn't know what they were talking about. And then it seemed very unfair when people believed it. You probably felt that people shouldn't talk that way. They weren't being truthful. The reason you felt that way is because God only wants you to tell the truth and to be fair.

When you choose integrity, people notice a difference. Some will love the choice you've made to follow Jesus. Others will try to prove that you're no different from anyone else. May those people "see the good way you have lived as a Christian" and feel ashamed when they say something about you that's not true.

- -

HELP ME SEEK INTEGRITY, GOD. HELP ME LEARN YOUR
PRINCIPLES AND LIVE THEM OUT. HELP ME TRUST YOU TO
SHOW PEOPLE THE TRUTH WHEN SOMEONE LIES ABOUT ME.

WALK IN HONOR

*How happy are the sons of a man who is
right with God and walks in honor!*
PROVERBS 20:7

People notice integrity. They observe some of your good choices but not every choice you make. Only you and God know all your choices, because nothing is hidden from God. He knows when you slip up and fail. He knows how hard making the right choice can be sometimes. And He knows your heart and knows why you made the choice you made—even when you may not understand it yourself.

Today's verse says that when you're more than brave you can show integrity by walking with God in a way that's right and honorable. You don't try to hide sins—*you admit them.* You don't try to tell everybody how wonderful you are—*you let your life look as much like Jesus as possible.* Be a boy of integrity and be satisfied, joyful, and forgiven.

- -

I KNOW YOU PAY ATTENTION WHENEVER I MAKE
A CHOICE, FATHER. HELP ME MAKE GOOD ONES.
HELP ME HONOR YOU WITH EVERY DECISION.

THE RIGHT CHOICE FIRST

*We want to do the right thing. We want God
and men to know we are honest.*
2 CORINTHIANS 8:21

Being a boy of integrity isn't easy. You struggle to have integrity on your own. God helps you make good choices and encourages you to leave bad choices behind. That's encouragement you need.

You want to do the right thing. Learn enough from God to make the right thing your first choice. Other times you need to pray and then accept His help to stay away from choices that cause people to think you aren't trustworthy.

The apostle Paul helped people learn about Jesus. He said that Christians should want to do the right thing. Those Christians wanted to be known for being honest. Maybe you do too. Brave boys are like that, you know.

- -

**I WANT TO DO THE RIGHT THING, GOD. AND IN THOSE TIMES
WHEN I'M NOT SURE, WOULD YOU HELP ME TO BE WISE
ENOUGH TO ASK FOR YOUR HELP? I WANT TO BE A BRAVE
BOY WHO TRUSTS YOU TO HELP ME DO THE RIGHT THING.**

NEW LIFE INTEGRITY

*Watch the path of your feet, and all your ways will
be sure. . . . Turn your foot away from sin.*
PROVERBS 4:26–27

Doing what you've always done is not really how God wants you to live life, but sometimes it just seems easier. The life you lived once upon a time didn't lead to integrity, and it didn't point you in the best direction. Going back to those choices today just wastes time because your spiritual feet are walking the wrong way.

Pay attention to where you're going. If it's not toward God, then you're not only going nowhere important, but you're actually refusing to spend time with God—and God wants to spend time with you.

Integrity depends on new choices, following a new plan with a new leader. It's choosing a good choice when making that choice is not something you used to do. Integrity means God's new life for you is finally making sense.

- -

I'M JUST ONE BOY AMONG MILLIONS, FATHER, YET YOU KNOW
ME, LOVE ME, AND CHOOSE TO WALK WITH ME EVERY DAY.
POINT MY FEET IN A DIRECTION THAT FOLLOWS YOU.
GROW THIS BOY INTO A MAN OF INTEGRITY.

INTEGRITY'S BEST VERSE

Christian brothers, keep your minds thinking about whatever is true, whatever is respected, whatever is right, whatever is pure, whatever can be loved, and whatever is well thought of. If there is anything good and worth giving thanks for, think about these things.
PHILIPPIANS 4:8

Today's verse is a perfect description of integrity. It lists all the good things that increase the strength of integrity. Think about what is true, not false. Think about what is respected, not sinful. Consider what is right, not wrong. Love what is pure, not spoiled. Choose love, not hate. Spend time learning more about excellent things, not things that waste your time. Good things and things that make you grateful are things you should let your mind explore.

Integrity is an impressive choice to make for boys who are brave. Brave boys are serious about a life that's been made so much better by the love of a very good God.

- -

MY MIND CAN WANDER, GOD. HELP ME TO KEEP THINKING ABOUT TRUTH, RESPECTABILITY, RIGHT LIVING, PURITY, LOVE, EXCELLENCE, GOODNESS, AND GRATITUDE. KEEP MY MIND THINKING ABOUT YOU AND THE THINGS THAT PLEASE YOU. HELP ME CHASE INTEGRITY.

TRUTH RECOGNITION

Do not lie to each other. You have put out of your life your old ways. You have now become a new person and are always learning more about Christ. You are being made more like Christ. He is the One Who made you.
COLOSSIANS 3:9–10

Lie long enough and you won't recognize truth. God wants you to tell the truth, look for truth, and make truth important. A trustworthy boy tells the truth because he wants his new life to keep moving in a good direction. Keep learning more about Jesus. His life has changed your future, and your future should show faithfulness to God. God's plan is to make you more like Jesus. That would be impossible to do if you didn't recognize the difference between the truth and a lie.

Trustworthy boys are brave because they tell the truth when it's hard, do what they say they will do when it would be easier to ignore the request, and follow God when it would be easier to watch from a distance.

BEING TRUSTWORTHY ISN'T EASY, FATHER. I'VE FAILED, AND I MAY FAIL AGAIN, BUT I WANT TO DO BETTER. YOU'VE PROMISED TO TEACH ME. HELP ME LEARN.

TRUST YOUR HEART?

He who trusts in his own heart is a fool.
PROVERBS 28:26

God said your heart will lie to you, and in today's verse He said that it's foolish to trust your heart. Being trustworthy is something different than trusting your heart. If your heart will fail to help you, then your trust cannot be in what *you* can do, but in what *God* has done for you. God's faithfulness can make your faithfulness grow. Your trust in Him is what can make you trustworthy. Why? Because you're relying on His teaching and instruction to help you make the best choices.

God is the only One who will ever be absolutely trustworthy. He can't lie, and He can't break a promise. He'll be faithful even when you aren't. He doesn't break promises even when you break His rules. Don't make a foolish mistake by trusting yourself more than you trust God.

- -

I CAN'T TRUST MY HEART, GOD. IT DOESN'T ALWAYS HAVE THE RIGHT ANSWERS. BUT YOU DO. HELP ME TO REMEMBER THAT YOU'RE TRUSTWORTHY WHEN I'M NOT. YOU'RE FAITHFUL—AND I WANT TO BE.

HIS LAWS PROTECT

"Do not tell a lie about your neighbor."
EXODUS 20:16

You can read one of God's laws and think you've uncovered another thing that you aren't supposed to do. It can seem like God is taking all kinds of choices away from you. The truth is you can tell a lie about someone—and you probably have—but some of the reasons that this is a sin is because it hurts the person you told a lie about, it causes others to look at that person in a way that's not true, and it keeps you from being considered trustworthy when people discover your lie.

God's laws don't hurt you—they protect you. When you do your best to live a life that shows compassion to other people, it improves your reputation, makes you more responsible, and allows you to become more faithful to the God who is truth.

- -

YOU DON'T LIE ABOUT ME, FATHER. YOU TELL ME MY HEART WILL LIE TO ME, THAT I WON'T BE AS TRUSTWORTHY AS YOU ARE. BUT THEN YOU TELL ME I CAN RELY ON YOU. I CAN TRUST YOUR HEART WHEN MINE IS DEFECTIVE. TEACH ME TO BE TRUSTWORTHY.

TRUTH TO TRUST

"Make them holy for Yourself by the truth. Your Word is truth."
JOHN 17:17

Early in this book, you read that God wants you to be holy, which means being set apart to do something He wants you to do. His truth sets you apart, but how does that happen? Reading the Bible sets you apart. That's not news—you've read that before in this very book. And now that you've been reading about being trustworthy, we can connect the links: God's Word is where you learn truth, truth is what you need to learn, learning means following, and following can make you trustworthy. So becoming trustworthy isn't like a switch that can be turned on and off whenever you feel like it; it's a process.

Learning God's truth helps you identify truth. When you are set apart, you are more likely to be trustworthy because you have become a student who follows the trustworthy God.

- -

THANKS FOR GIVING ME TRUTH THAT DOESN'T CHANGE, GOD. HELP ME READ SO I KNOW, HEAR SO I REMEMBER, AND SPEAK SO OTHERS CAN HEAR THAT YOU'RE THAT IMPORTANT.

HE DOESN'T HIDE

Those who know Your name will put their trust in You. For You, O Lord, have never left alone those who look for You.
PSALM 9:10

God isn't the "man upstairs" or just a "higher power." Everything you see exists because God said it should. He may seem mysterious, but He can be known. When you really understand who God is, it's easy to trust Him.

Look for God, for He can be found. He doesn't hide from those who seek Him. He doesn't run from those who chase. He loves you and wants you to know Him.

God is trustworthy. You can trust Him with your dreams and hopes and even your questions. Questions show you're curious to know more about Him and His dreams and hopes, and even His questions. He's curious and wants to hear from you *about you*.

It's always a good time to trust a very personal God.

- -

GIVE ME THE STRENGTH TO CHASE AFTER YOU, FATHER.
GIVE ME A MIND THAT WANTS TO KNOW MORE ABOUT
YOU. GIVE ME THE COURAGE TO SHARE EVERYTHING ABOUT
ME. YOUR LOVE HELPS ME GROW TO LOVE YOU TOO.

THE INVITATION

The works of His hands are faithful and right. All His Laws are true.

PSALM 111:7

What if God took time away from helping you because He was just too tired and needed a break? That won't ever happen. God never posts a note saying He'll be back after lunch. He won't plan a vacation to get away from it all. He loves you too much to leave you without His care.

Everything He does is right, and He does everything because He is trustworthy and faithful. He gave laws that show what He's like and how He'd like for you to live.

Because God never breaks His own law, you can expect Him to love you—*all the time*; to be compassionate—*without a break*; and trustworthy—*without any reminder*.

Even when you can't follow His laws 100 percent of the time, He will. And He invites you to accept His help in living a new life. If you're brave, you'll accept His invitation.

- -

THANK YOU FOR NEVER BEING TOO TIRED TO HELP ME, GOD. I WILL FAIL, BUT YOU NEVER DO. YOU PAY ATTENTION WHEN I NEED HELP. YOU HEAR WHEN I CALL. THANKS FOR NEVER TAKING A BREAK FROM ME.

OUT OF CONTROL

A man who cannot rule his own spirit is like
a city whose walls are broken down.
PROVERBS 25:28

In those moments when you're out of control, you're left in a dangerous situation. A couple of stories in the Bible help to explain this. The first is about a city called Jericho. When the walls were destroyed, an army took over the city. The second story is about a city called Jerusalem that came back from destruction once the walls were rebuilt.

God can use these stories to show how important it is to have protection. God protects you, and He has given you tools to provide protection. One of those is *self-control*. It's kind of like an inner soldier standing guard over choices that can be made. When you have self-control, you'll be more likely to make the right choices.

- -

I NEED TO PAY ATTENTION TO WHAT'S HAPPENING, FATHER. I WANT TO BE BRAVE ENOUGH TO USE THE PROTECTIVE SELF-CONTROL YOU GIVE ME. LIVING OUT OF CONTROL WILL ALWAYS LEAD ME TO MAKE OUT-OF-CONTROL CHOICES.

THOUGHT PERMISSION

You must be the boss over your mind.
1 PETER 4:7

The mind God gave you is meant to help you think, ask questions, and make good choices. You must be in control of your mind because it can be bossy and want its way. It may also try to make you worried and scared. Sometimes it does a really good job of both.

The Bible says your mind is supposed to obey you—not the other way around. Examine each thought you think to see if it should stay. A lot of thoughts don't belong and can cause damage if you allow them to stay. Some thoughts can even tell you to do something you wouldn't normally think of doing, and you'll do those things and suffer the consequences.

God can restore right thinking and clean your heart. You don't have to do something just because the idea spent time in your mind. Be careful what you give your mind permission to think.

- -

I WANT TO MAKE GOOD CHOICES, GOD. ALL CHOICES START IN WHAT I THINK ABOUT. HELP ME CHOOSE GOOD THOUGHTS SO I CAN MAKE THE BEST CHOICES.

WHO ASKS YOU TO SIN?

You have never been tempted to sin in any different way than other people. God is faithful. He will not allow you to be tempted more than you can take. But when you are tempted, He will make a way for you to keep from falling into sin.
1 CORINTHIANS 10:13

Once you know that you can be boss over your mind, you should understand how God helps. God will never tempt you. He'll never ask you to break His rules just so He can catch you sinning. But His enemy, Satan, *will* try to get you to break God's law. When that happens, God will step in and offer a choice that doesn't involve breaking His law. You'll have to decide if you'll do what God says or make a choice that God would never make.

God will also protect you from making bad choices. God doesn't want you to be so tempted that you can't hear His way out.

- -

YOUR FAITHFULNESS CAN LEAD ME THROUGH HARD AND UNHELPFUL CHOICES, FATHER. YOU ALWAYS PROVIDE A CORRECT CHOICE THAT HELPS ME AND PLEASES YOU.

GUARD DUTY

*Keep awake! Watch at all times. The
devil is working against you.*
1 PETER 5:8

Yesterday you learned that God's enemy, Satan, doesn't want to see you succeed. Today you have read that this enemy will always work against you. It is his voice you hear when you break God's law. He tells you that God could never accept someone like you, *but He has*. Satan tells you that God could never love someone like you, *but He does*. Satan says you can never be forgiven, *but God says you can.*

The best thing you can do is pay attention and look for times when Satan drops in to tempt or accuse. He is not your friend. He never will be. He loves to see brave boys fail, and he hopes that your failure keeps you from coming back to God. When you are accused, it's not God who is accusing you. God waits because He wants to spend time with you. He doesn't condemn, because He wants to see you find truth and let it change your direction.

- -

RECOGNIZING THE DIFFERENCE IN HOW YOU AND YOUR ENEMY RESPOND TO ME IS IMPORTANT, GOD. HELP ME TO LISTEN TO YOU.

A TEMPER LOST

A fool always loses his temper, but a wise man keeps quiet.
PROVERBS 29:11

If you have lost your temper, then self-control probably found a place to hide while you made that choice. If you chose to keep quiet when someone made you mad, then self-control showed up and was directing "thought traffic" in your mind like a police officer. God calls it foolish to lose your temper.

You might think you have good reason to be angry, but when you get angry—and stay angry—you do things you don't normally do, say things you don't normally say, and think thoughts you have trouble controlling.

Be brave. Control your choices. Don't say the mean thing that your mind insists that you say. It really is all about choices that you get to make because you're learning what God wants. God's way out is always worth taking.

WORDS CAN HURT, FATHER. I DON'T LIKE TO HURT, AND I ALSO DON'T WANT TO HURT OTHERS. WHEN SOMEONE SAYS SOMETHING MEAN TO ME, MAYBE THEY'VE BEEN HURT. YOU GIVE ME THE CHOICE TO STOP THE HURTING. THEN I CAN COME TO YOU FOR HEALING.

THINGS GOD DIDN'T SEND

For God did not give us a spirit of fear. He gave us a
spirit of power and of love and of a good mind.
2 TIMOTHY 1:7

Fear is a pretty big enemy of self-control. Worry isn't a gift God sent. Anxiety isn't something God wants you to keep. You were given gifts that change how you respond to fear. God gave you love, and that sends fear away. He gave you strength, and that makes you brave. He gave you a good mind, and that will help you keep the important information in your mind and send the unimportant things away.

It's kind of a big deal to know what God did not send so you can recognize what He does send. God doesn't send things like despair, cruelty, unfaithfulness, lies, depression, pride, or criticism. Sure, these things exist, but they don't come from God. Aren't you glad God sends good gifts?

- -

FATHER, HELP ME TO BE THANKFUL FOR THE VERY GOOD GIFTS THAT WERE MEANT FOR ME TO RECOGNIZE, USE, AND SHARE.

PERSEVERE

I pray that God's great power will make you strong, and that you will have joy as you wait and do not give up.
COLOSSIANS 1:11

Pray for other people. Ask God to make them strong, brave, and courageous. You are learning to be brave and how to grow after becoming brave. Now what? Pray that the same joy you experience will be something other people experience. The way to keep bravery close is to persevere, to be willing to wait for the things God has promised.

Perseverance is a lot like hope. It knows that God can be trusted. It does what God asks. It believes that what will happen in the future is worth waiting for today.

Perseverance is living through struggle because you know there's a better story waiting. It can help make you strong because it's part of God's big story.

- -

YOU KNOW WHAT IT'S LIKE TO PERSEVERE, FATHER. YOU'VE HAD TO ENDURE THE WRONG CHOICES THAT PEOPLE MAKE FOR A LOT LONGER THAN I'VE BEEN ALIVE. YET YOU DON'T GIVE UP. HELP ME TO PERSEVERE IN MY STRUGGLES AND TO SEE THEM AS SOMETHING THAT HELPS ME GET CLOSE TO YOU.

STRUGGLES FACED

We think of those who stayed true to Him as
happy even though they suffered.
JAMES 5:11

There have been many missionaries who faced struggles as they went to other nations to tell people about Jesus. There have been many preachers who have shared Jesus and have been ridiculed and hurt for sharing the very best message. The Bible tells about a man named Stephen who talked about Jesus and was killed. All of these brave people would say that their greatest satisfaction in life was telling people about Jesus. They were willing to endure hard days if it meant someone could finally hear about the type of love only God offers.

Perseverance involves living through, struggling with, and overcoming obstacles in life. There is satisfaction in knowing that someday the worst will be behind you. It may not be any fun to make the choice to persevere, but perseverance means there's a finish line.

- -

REACHING THE END OF ANY STRUGGLE MAKES ME HAPPY, GOD. IT MEANS YOU HELPED ME DO WHAT I COULDN'T DO ON MY OWN. I'M GRATEFUL FOR YOUR COMPANY IN MY STRUGGLE.

CARRY NO EXTRAS

Let us put every thing out of our lives that keeps us from doing what we should. Let us keep running in the race that God has planned for us.

HEBREWS 12:1

Let's say you're asked to run in a race. You feel pretty good because you're a good runner. You like feeling wind in your face and pounding the ground beneath your feet. On race day you're ready, but you choose to carry a backpack filled with snacks, water, and some sandwiches in case you get hungry. Oh, and there's a dog you want to drop off along the race course (he likes to be carried). With your free hand you lug a heavy bag of groceries for a stop along the route. You look around and notice that no one else is carrying these extras. You think all this stuff will affect how fast you can run—*and you're right.*

That's the picture of today's verse. Don't take things you don't need when running the race of life. God will take care of your needs.

- -

FATHER, IT'S HARD TO ENDURE WHEN I INSIST ON CARRYING WHAT YOU SAY I SHOULD LET GO OF. HELP ME LET GO OF THE EXTRA STUFF, AND HELP ME PERSEVERE IN LIFE'S RACE.

PERSONAL BEST

You must run so you will win the crown.
1 CORINTHIANS 9:24

You've probably heard the term *personal best*. It means, for example, that every time you run the same distance, you try to beat your best time. It's kind of like a race against yourself. You compete against what you've done before and not against what others are doing now.

The race God wants you to run is against yourself. If you think of your Christian life as a race, then you might think that trying to beat other people by doing more good things more often is what God is talking about. He wants you to pray for and help others—but to run against yourself.

God loves everyone, is willing to rescue anyone, and wants your choices to be your "personal best." Run, persevere, and finish the race that God intends just for you.

- -

YOU DON'T WANT ME TO THINK OF MYSELF AS BETTER THAN ANYONE ELSE, GOD. THIS IS BECAUSE YOU WANT ME TO LOVE THEM AND NOT TRY TO MAKE THEM FEEL BAD. MAKE MY JOURNEY ALL ABOUT FOLLOWING YOU THE BEST WAY POSSIBLE BECAUSE I'M WILLING TO DO WHAT YOU ASK ME TO DO.

ON THE WAY

May the Lord lead your hearts into the love of
God. May He help you as you wait for Christ.

2 THESSALONIANS 3:5

Going to the dentist or doctor can be hard. You sit in the waiting room with people you don't know, looking at books or magazines that might have been on the table since before you were born. If you're lucky, there might be an aquarium with a few goldfish to entertain you. Waiting is hard because there are so many other things you want to do, and the fact that it's a doctor or dentist visit you're waiting for doesn't seem very fun either.

Waiting for Jesus may sometimes feel a bit like being in a waiting room. You live through stuff you don't want to have to go through with people you might not enjoy being around, and you read a Bible that was written before you were born.

But waiting for Jesus can also make you think about what's next. If you are His brave child, you have nothing to dread. Anticipating His return can bring joy and peace. Persevere a little longer. God's best is on the way.

- -

WAITING FOR YOU SHOULD BE DIFFERENT, JESUS. I NEED
TO REMEMBER THAT MY STRUGGLES WILL BE OVER
WHEN YOU COME. NOW, THAT IS SOMETHING
TO LOOK FORWARD TO! MAY I PERSEVERE
PATIENTLY AS I WATCH AND WAIT FOR YOU.

TESTS

My Christian brothers, you should be happy
when you have all kinds of tests. You know these
prove your faith. It helps you not to give up.
JAMES 1:2–3

Perseverance is a good thing. It helps you understand life's race. It helps you notice the struggles that people face during the race. It reminds you that there's an end to the race so that you won't want to give up.

Sure, you've read that before in this very book. The hope you have in Jesus means you're looking forward to a big finish. When you persevere to the finish of your struggle, you're sending out a message that says, "God can be trusted. I trusted Him, and He helped me through some pretty hard tests. He'll help you too."

- -

SOMETIMES I WISH I DIDN'T HAVE TO GO THROUGH SO MANY TESTS, GOD. THEY MAKE ME TIRED. BUT YOU GIVE ME STRENGTH, AND YOU'RE TRUSTWORTHY. HELP ME, PLEASE, TO PERSEVERE. I DON'T WANT TO GIVE UP.

TELL HIM

If we tell Him our sins, He is faithful and we can depend on Him to forgive us of our sins. He will make our lives clean.
1 JOHN 1:9

God wants you to be honest enough to tell Him when you break one of His rules. You can't hide that kind of information from God, so it just makes sense to tell Him. Telling God will not make Him mad at you. The Bible says that He is faithful and dependable to do one very important thing—forgive you when you tell Him all about what He already knows. This is a sign of bravery.

Usually, when you break a rule you might get punished. God chooses instead to forgive, and then He gives you a way to move in a better direction. You may still face consequences for breaking His rules, but He doesn't get angry when you tell Him the truth about your sins.

- -

YOU CAN MAKE MY LIFE CLEAN, FATHER, BUT I HAVE TO STOP HIDING FIRST. YOU CAN FORGIVE ME, BUT I NEED TO TELL YOU WHAT I'VE DONE. YOU ARE DEPENDABLE, BUT I HAVE TO DEPEND ON YOU.

THE END OF FORGIVENESS

Then Peter came to Jesus and said, "Lord, how many times may my brother sin against me and I forgive him, up to seven times?" Jesus said to him, "I tell you, not seven times but seventy times seven!"
MATTHEW 18:21–22

Do you forgive other people when they do something that hurts you? If so, that's pretty awesome. Do you count how many times you forgive? If so, that's not so unusual. Do you think there should be an end to your forgiveness if they keep it up? If so, you might understand this story about Jesus' disciple Peter.

Peter had been hearing a lot about forgiveness. It would have been better if he kept listening to Jesus, but he wanted to impress his Teacher. He asked Jesus when he could stop offering forgiveness. He thought he was being generous by offering to forgive seven times. Jesus pretty much told him to forgive—and to stop counting.

- -

YOU FORGIVE ME, GOD. YOU WANT ME TO FORGIVE OTHERS. YOU DON'T WANT ME TO LOOK FORWARD TO A MOMENT WHEN I NO LONGER NEED TO FORGIVE SOMEONE. YOU'VE NEVER STOPPED FORGIVING ME. I AM GRATEFUL.

FORGIVENESS IS POSSIBLE

Try to understand other people. Forgive each other. If you have something against someone, forgive him.
COLOSSIANS 3:13

Because you've been hurt by things other people say and do, then you should remember that other people are hurt by things someone said or did to them. You might be able to do some of the things you've read in this book. You might be able to hold your tongue, pray for those who hurt you, or show kindness.

Some people don't know enough about God to make this good choice. That's why God asks *you* to forgive. Some people need to see that forgiveness is possible. Some might be able to make that choice when they know God.

When you understand that people will act in ways to show they need God when they do things that need to be forgiven, it will give you the chance to forgive, pray for them, and share God's love with them.

- -

FORGIVENESS IS A GIFT I CAN ACCEPT, AND IT'S A GIFT I CAN GIVE, FATHER. HELP ME UNDERSTAND PEOPLE WELL ENOUGH TO FORGIVE THEM. I NEEDED YOU, AND NOW I KNOW THEY NEED YOU TOO.

NOT WHAT THEY EXPECT

[Jesus said,] "I say to you who hear Me, love those who work against you. Do good to those who hate you."
LUKE 6:27

It's possible to think that God should forgive you because you're really sorry for breaking His law. It's also possible to think that God shouldn't forgive some people because you're pretty sure they aren't really sorry. When you think that way, you might just be trying to take God's job. He doesn't need your help, but you will need His.

When someone does something to hurt you, do something that helps them. When they do things that make life hard for you, show them love in return. That's not what they expect, and it can leave them thinking.

Forgiveness is more than just asking God to forgive you. It's making sure no one has a reason to see you as unforgivable or unwilling to forgive.

- -

SOMETIMES IT SEEMS UNFAIR TO FORGIVE SOMEONE WHO HAS HURT ME, GOD. THEN I REMEMBER THAT EVERY DAY YOU FORGIVE PEOPLE WHO HAVE HURT YOU. WOULD YOU HELP ME TO FORGIVE THOSE WHO HURT ME?

FORGOTTEN?

"I will not remember their sins and wrong-doings anymore."
HEBREWS 10:17

God does something for you that you can't do for others no matter how hard you try. God not only can forgive you, but He can forget your sin ever happened. You can't do that. You might want to, but you can't tell your mind to forget something and then never remember it again. Memories of the hurt you have felt can come up at any time, even when you didn't plan on thinking about it.

The one thing you can do is choose to forgive and never use the memory of the pain to punish the other person. When you want to store the information away to use against them, then it just means you are planning to do something that will need to be forgiven. You don't have to do this. God doesn't want you to do this.

- -

HELP ME LIVE A LIFE THAT FORGIVES BECAUSE I'VE BEEN FORGIVEN, FATHER. HELP ME STOP MAKING PEOPLE PAY FOR HURTING ME ONCE I FORGIVE THEM.

DON'T WASTE TIME

"Forgive us our sins as we forgive those who sin against us."
MATTHEW 6:12

The Bible talks a lot about the gift of forgiveness and the joy of being forgiven. Forgiveness sets things right side up, cleans the record of sin, and restores friendship. Those are all really good things, and it's why it just makes sense to follow God's example.

Be brave enough to show mercy (more on that in the next devotion) and forgive. This is a brave choice, because when you demand justice, you don't know when to stop asking for the other person to repay, forgiveness is no longer a gift, and things stay complicated.

Jesus wants you to believe that you can ask Him to forgive and He will. He wants you to trust that He can help you forgive others even when they don't know they should ask.

- -

I WANT TO BE FORGIVEN, GOD. I WANT TO KNOW THAT THINGS ARE GOING TO BE OKAY. HELP ME TO BE BRAVE ENOUGH TO FORGIVE BECAUSE I DON'T WANT TO FEEL BITTER AND KEEP REMEMBERING EVERYTHING THAT EVERYONE HAS EVER DONE TO ME. I DON'T WANT TO WASTE MY TIME AND ENERGY ON UNFORGIVENESS.

MERCY

*"You must have loving-kindness just as
your Father has loving-kindness."*
LUKE 6:36

The next few days are all about mercy. In the verses shared, you should remember that loving-kindness and mercy mean the same thing.

When your mom says that if you don't do your homework you'll miss out on something that you really want to do, you'll probably think it's a good idea to do your homework. You heard the rule, and it made sense to follow it. What if you didn't follow the rule? What if the homework didn't get done? The consequence for breaking the rule was the loss of the fun you'd planned. You broke the rules. But let's say your mom decides not to keep you from the event. That's mercy.

Mercy is when you deserve a penalty but then you're not penalized. God shows mercy to people who break His rules but then turn from their sin and ask for His forgiveness.

I'VE ALWAYS NEEDED YOUR MERCY, FATHER, EVEN THOUGH I HAVE DONE NOTHING TO DESERVE IT. THANK YOU FOR FORGIVING ME AND PUTTING ME IN RIGHT STANDING WITH YOU.

MERCY FOLLOWS FORGIVENESS

Anyone who shows no loving-kindness will have no loving-kindness shown to him when he is told he is guilty. But if you show loving-kindness, God will show loving-kindness to you when you are told you are guilty.

JAMES 2:13

You probably remember that God wants you to forgive as He has forgiven you, and that mercy comes after forgiveness. But when you refuse to forgive, you cannot show mercy. And when you won't show mercy, other people may not show mercy to you when they know you're guilty of breaking the rules.

Show mercy, kindness, and love, and it will often mean that God will show you mercy, kindness, and love when you've broken the rules. His mercy follows His forgiveness. His love shows kindness. It's what God offers, and it's exactly what you need.

You might even remember that God doesn't ask you to do what He will not do. His mercy is why you can be merciful.

- -

I CAN SHOW KINDNESS BECAUSE YOU SHOW ME HOW, FATHER. I CAN SHOW MERCY BECAUSE YOU HAVE BEEN MERCIFUL. HELP ME TO DO WHAT YOU'VE ALREADY DONE.

MERCY WISE

"Those who show loving-kindness are happy, because they will have loving-kindness shown to them."
MATTHEW 5:7

Showing mercy is a brave thing to do, but it's also wise. You could think that if you forgive and don't expect someone to pay for hurting you that you've just agreed to something that isn't fair—*and you'd be right.* This issue isn't about being fair; it's about being kinder or more merciful than you need to be. When you do something like that, you're giving people a preview of what God is like. He gives gifts not because they are deserved but because people need things like love, forgiveness, and mercy. He gives and doesn't expect payment for His gifts.

Show mercy to others, and you'll be happy knowing that you'll receive mercy at just the right time. God loves to give mercy to those who show mercy.

- -

I WANT TO BE BRAVE ENOUGH AND WISE ENOUGH TO SHOW MERCY, FATHER. HELP ME SEE YOUR MERCY AS MY BEST EXAMPLE, AND THEN LET THERE BE JUST THE RIGHT TIMES TO SHOW MERCY BECAUSE YOU'RE MERCIFUL TO ME.

THE GOOD CHOICE

*"Go and understand these words, 'I want loving-kindness
and not a gift to be given.' For I have not come to call good
people. I have come to call those who are sinners."*
MATTHEW 9:13

God isn't looking for some kind of payment for your sins. Jesus
has already paid the price for your forgiveness on the cross. What
He desires is a repentant heart, a heart that turns away from
sin and turns toward God. He wants you to make good choices
more than He wants to hear that you're sorry. That doesn't mean
He won't forgive; He absolutely will. He just wants you to grow
in your Christian life rather than repeating a cycle of sinning,
trying to pay for your own sin, and then saying you're sorry. You
can ask Him to help you make better choices from the start.

I DON'T KNOW WHY IT'S SO HARD TO MAKE GOOD CHOICES,
GOD. HELP ME TO REMEMBER THAT I SHOULD NEVER LEAVE
YOU OUT WHEN MAKING ANY CHOICE. AND I DON'T WANT TO
GET CAUGHT UP IN TRYING TO PAY FOR MY OWN SINS WHEN
I SHOULD BE TRUSTING IN YOUR MERCY INSTEAD. JESUS PAID
FOR MY FORGIVENESS. MY JOB IS JUST TO TRUST IN HIM.

DON'T TRY TO HIDE

Go with complete trust to the throne of God. We will receive His loving-kindness and have His loving-favor to help us whenever we need it.

HEBREWS 4:16

No waiting. No line. No delay. God is ready to meet you. Go to Him and trust that His mercy is more than enough to make a difference. Ask Him for help, and He will help.

You don't have to be afraid of God. Don't even try to hide from Him. Don't run away. Trust God enough to come to Him. He has been waiting to hear from you. He loves you enough to offer mercy, which you don't deserve and can't earn. Mercy is His gift.

Don't forget to use your thankful voice to let God know you recognize that He has given an amazing gift and you're happy to receive it. His everyday mercies are new, fresh, and incredible.

- -

YOU PROBABLY WONDER WHY I WAIT SO LONG TO TALK TO YOU, FATHER. THAT'S FAIR. I SOMETIMES TRY TO WORK THINGS OUT ON MY OWN. HELP ME TO REMEMBER THAT I CAN SAVE TIME IF I WILL JUST COME TO YOU FIRST.

LET GOD HANDLE THE DETAILS

It is because of the Lord's loving-kindness that we
are not destroyed for His loving-pity never ends. It
is new every morning. He is so very faithful.
LAMENTATIONS 3:22–23

God said that if you were to be paid for sinning, then your payment is death. That sounds pretty harsh, but God is perfect, and you can never pay the price for sin. That's why God sent Jesus. He paid because you couldn't. It's because of what Jesus did on the cross that mercy came into your life. Because of mercy, there's no talk of punishment. God was faithful to offer mercy, and you recognize His love because of mercy.

Be brave enough to give what you have been given. When others do wrong to you, forgive them. You can show mercy because you have met mercy.

- -

MERCY IS AN ADVENTURE THAT COMES WITH A SURPRISE,
GOD. I DON'T EXPECT TO SEE MERCY, AND MAYBE THAT'S
WHY I'M SURPRISED BY IT WHEN YOU GIVE IT TO ME. THANK
YOU FOR LOVE I DIDN'T EARN, MERCY THAT I CAN SHARE,
AND FAITHFULNESS THAT HELPS ME TRUST.

FOLLOW THE LEADER

"Whoever wants to be great among you, let him care for you."
MATTHEW 20:26

A brave boy like you could be a leader. *Seriously.* Practice all the things you've learned in this book and you'll be walking the road of leadership. No, it doesn't mean you demand that people do what you want. It doesn't mean you get to make the rules. Today's verse says that being a leader means caring for other people, looking out for them, and treating them with respect.

If you want to be more than brave, then follow the Leader so you can learn to lead. That is what God wants for you. The kind of leader He wants is someone who can inspire others to follow Him. Someone who cares more about what God wants than what they want. This kind of leader follows God before he leads others. Be that kind of brave. Be that kind of leader.

- -

I'M WILLING TO FOLLOW YOU, FATHER, AND YOU'RE WILLING TO LEAD. HELP ME LEAD WHEN YOU WANT ME TO LEAD, AND HELP ME TO REMEMBER WHAT LEADING MEANS.

DO WHAT HE DID

"You should do as I have done to you."
JOHN 13:15

If Jesus had been mean and filled with hate, and if Jesus had made those who hated Him pay, could He have told the men and women who followed Him, "Do as I have done"?

When you follow the Leader, if you're supposed to do what He has done for you, then you have some good decisions to make. Jesus made brave decisions every day. He still does. Love like He loves. Forgive because He forgives. Be kind because He's kind. Be faithful. Then what? Be humble, thankful, and good. Be honest and generous, and persevere. Look back through the pages of this book and find even more that you can do because of what Jesus has already done.

Read the Bible and discover stories of wisdom, perseverance, and initiative. Being brave isn't the end of a journey; it's a fantastic beginning.

I WANT TO BE LIKE YOUR SON, GOD. THAT MEANS I HAVE SOME HOMEWORK TO DO. HELP ME LEARN WHAT I NEED TO LEARN TO BE MORE LIKE THE LEADER YOU MADE ME TO BE.

BECOME A TEACHER

Do your best to know that God is pleased with you.
Be as a workman who has nothing to be ashamed
of. Teach the words of truth in the right way.

2 TIMOTHY 2:15

Being a leader means knowing where you're going. Who wants to follow someone who's lost? Be brave enough to learn, brave enough to follow God, and brave enough to lead people to Him.

God wants you to be a student, but He also wants you to become a teacher. He doesn't want you to worry that you're too young or not smart enough. Learn and share what you've learned. Don't add anything to it, and don't subtract any of the truth from what you learn. What you share must be God's truth and not what you think it should be. That's why you need to "teach the words of truth in the right way."

Follow. Learn. Lead.

- -

I DON'T WANT YOU TO BE ASHAMED OF ME WHEN I TELL PEOPLE ABOUT YOU, FATHER. I NEED ENOUGH WISDOM TO KNOW HOW, WHEN, AND WHERE TO SHARE YOUR VERY BEST NEWS. HELP ME TO SEE HOW IMPORTANT IT IS TO KNOW MORE ABOUT YOU.

LEADERSHIP PURITY

*Keep your heart pure for out of it are
the important things of life.*
PROVERBS 4:23

The leader God knows you can be will be wonderful. This leader will be brave, kind, and pure.

You've read about purity in this book, but let's look at this from the big window of leadership. Being a leader for God means that you do your best to keep your heart pure. That requires making really good choices and never waiting to tell God about the times when you made a less than pure choice.

Why is purity important to leaders? God says that important things happen when purity is your choice. Purity boosts your reputation (the way people think of you). Purity means you're taking your friendship with God seriously. Purity is a way to show that you're faithful to God in the way that you lead.

PURITY IS MORE THAN A GOOD IDEA, GOD. HELP ME TO SEE THE IMPORTANCE OF FOLLOWING YOUR LAWS. HELP ME TO OBEY WHAT THE BIBLE TELLS ME TO DO. HELP ME LEAD IN A WAY THAT OTHERS UNDERSTAND THAT YOU HAVE THE MOST IMPORTANT PLACE IN MY LIFE.

WAITING FOR YOU TO RESPOND

Give your way over to the Lord. Trust in Him also.
PSALM 37:5

Today you can stop trying to be in control of everything. It's superhard work and something only God has ever done successfully.

Can you control what other people do? *No.* Can you control the weather? *No.* Can you make your friends do only what you want them to do? *No.*

You can control the way you react to things. You can have control over the choices you make. You can control how seriously you take following God.

God is waiting for you to remember that He controls everything. He tells the sun when to rise and set. He tells the clouds when to form. He decided how He would rescue you, and then He waited for you to respond.

You will be the best leader when you let Him lead you first.

- -

I WANT TO BE ABLE TO CONTROL MY CHOICES AND LET YOU CONTROL MY FUTURE, FATHER. I WANT TO LEARN TO MAKE THE CHOICES YOU WOULD MAKE. HELP ME TRUST YOU ENOUGH TO LET YOU TAKE ME TO THE BEST PLACES.

MOVE BEYOND

*"Do not fear, for I am with you. Do not be afraid,
for I am your God. I will give you strength, and
for sure I will help you. Yes, I will hold you up
with My right hand that is right and good."*
ISAIAH 41:10

One hundred and eighty pages of encouragement. That's what you'll have read when you get to the last word of this page. On each of these pages, you've read at least one thing about taking bravery and moving beyond courage to the things that send you on a quest.

God has planned many things for you, but very few of those things will happen if you don't follow Him. When you follow Him, you can lead others to Him. You can take every part of the mercy, kindness, and love that you've learned and introduce people you know to a God who is faithful, forgiving, and wise. You can be more than brave.

- -

**I HAVE LEARNED, AND I WILL KEEP LEARNING, GOD. I DO NOT WANT
TO BE AFRAID. YOU ARE THE GOD WHO GIVES ME STRENGTH.
YOU CAN HELP ME. I WILL ALWAYS NEED YOUR HELP.**

SCRIPTURE INDEX